EMOTIONAL
REVOLUTION = EVOLUTION

Releasing Shame/Guilt

LOIS HOLLIS

The Reading Glass Books
1-888-420-3050
www.readingglassbooks.com
fulfillment@readingglassbooks.com

CONTENTS

PERSONAL NOTE TO YOU
FOREWORD
DEFINITIONS

PART 1

PART 2

PART 3

Emotional Revolution = Evolution
RELEASING SHAME/GUILT

Lois Hollis

The Reading Glass Books

Dedicated
to the innate resilience
and
goodness we all have within us.

PERSONAL NOTE TO YOU

> "We touch the divine within ourselves
> when we allow our minds to
> disbelieve
> the SHAME/GUILT messages
> and
> believe
> in our unlimited potential."[1]

I present my book to educate, encourage, and empower you to live your life as your own. I openly share my findings on emotional healing that I have discovered. My information is contrary to the present opinions on shame and guilt because we need to redefine these two offenders of consciousness. I suggest that you initially allow this new information to spark your interest rather than reject it. Your open mind will allow you time to process any skepticism. Often SHAME/GUILT can create doubt, and you may lose focus while reading this book. This reaction is normal and means that your mind needs time to adjust to a greater knowledge. I encourage you to re-read this book, especially those chapters that speak to you, to help liberate yourself from the collective SHAME/GUILT hypnosis. Ultimately, you will learn how to enjoy a life that can fulfill your personal desires as well as your career goals.

---

[1]   Lois Hollis

FOREWORD

"One does not become enlightened by imagining figures of light, but my making the darkness conscious." Carl Jung

Anyone who has the foresight to pick up "Emotional Revolution = Evolution" is a person who has a yearning for a more joyous and graceful state of being in different aspects of their life. Lois Hollis explains concepts and patterns concerning shame and guilt that have previously been unexpressed even in psychology and spirituality, which is bound to help most anyone on their unique path to joy and freedom.

We are all beings of light, and yet so many of us find ourselves thrust into the darkness from our early years, partly from ideas and emotions that society and our families unknowingly leave upon us. The way from darkness to light is not intrinsically hard, but the many layers of guilt and shame that we have accepted along the way make it tricky indeed. As happened to me on my spiritual path, my mind was using spirituality to cover my sense of inadequacy rather than as a means to liberation. Many inspired teachers brought me out of this phase; Lois being one of the most important ones. The purer the teacher, the more effectively they can help you understand and transcend these negative forces that Lois has so adroitly pinned as SHAME/GUILT.

Lois has been to me many things. She inspired me with her first elegant work "The Universe Speaks", and I have been helped immensely by her 'life coaching' at a very critical period in my life. Truly, having enjoyed her first book, it was with great eagerness and anticipation that I read through her newest book. I was thrilled to see that Lois continued to grow and evolve her passion to new heights. What better teacher and guide can a person have than one who walked the long and winding path successfully to emerge stronger, happier, and with an unshakable sense of peace. Lois is such a gifted individual. When the darkness of her early childhood confronted her, she not only was able to face and understand it but created a system that can be of great help to us the readers.

Lois has brought to light the metaphorical 'darkness' that Carl Jung talked about almost a century ago. She so clearly defines it in this book as the hidden duo of Shame and Guilt or SHAME/GUILT that is possibly the biggest stumbling block to our emotional freedom. As you read this work, you will find yourself getting clearer on what these forces are and how extensively they influence your life. Moreover, with this knowledge you have the power to heal the past and move forward to live your life fully without fear.

Dr. Thomas Alexander, MD.

DEFINITIONS

SHAME/GUILT is the cycle of shame and guilt.

SHAME/GUILT BOND is a connection that joins the repressed SHAME/GUILT of one person to another. The size of the individual's repression controls the intensity of the bond.

SHAME/GUILT TRIGGER is a stimulus either of a particular word, behavior or sense that activates the physical and emotional reflex response similar to our initial SHAME/GUILT incident.

SHAME/GUILT SCAR is an imprint of SHAME/GUILT produced from our first abusive incident. The imprint scars our inner self, and it subsequently acts as an irritant within us to trigger the inappropriate responses we often re-experience from any new but similar abusive event.

SHAME/GUILT REPRESSION is a part of our personality that contains unresolved abusive events. It can also be called our **SHAME/GUILT HANDICAP** because it predisposes us to excessive guilt, abuse, failure, resentment, protracted grief, judgments, and other dysfunctional behaviors. Its density and size depend on the severity and number of unresolved issues. Our handicap becomes more likely to produce dysfunctional behavior the times that it outweighs our ethical sense. It creates the narcissistic and victim tendencies that obstruct our creative gifts and innate wisdom. It explains why even the best intentions do not always produce the desired results. The SHAME/GUILT repression or handicap is the accumulation of:

- self-defenses
- negative emotions
- self-recrimination
- emotional triggers
- unresolved traumatic events
- beliefs made from abusive experiences
- imprinting or influence from ancestors, family, and society
- SHAME/GUILT accumulated from abusers and abusive events

PART ONE

SHAME /GUILT DOMINANCE

CHAPTER ONE

THE BEGINNING

I HAD TO WRITE THIS BOOK

> "Change the future by changing the present.
> Change the present by healing the past."[2]

Each day as the morning sun greeted me through the flowing white curtains of my window, I greeted the SHAME/GUILT leech. Yes, SHAME/GUILT clung to me like a thirsty leech. I am Lois, and I was another abuse victim struggling to fend off melancholy and depression. My journey of feelings began in 1984 when I could no longer escape the mortification of guilt. My experiences, however, led me to go beyond the classic psychological approach for coping with childhood abuse; I healed and went on to support others to do the same. I believe that SHAME/GUILT poses as one of the greatest threats to our health and survival. I also believe that no event is too painful or sad to heal, no matter when we encounter it.

Prior to my collapse into SHAME/GUILT, l had fun in my early adult life. I made it so. My enthusiastic personality blossomed from memories of swinging on swings and making sandcastles on the beach. With Herculean efforts, I could escape my childhood traumas. Denial and a twenty-year marathon of headache pills came to my rescue, enabling me to repress those memories and rationalize artificial euphoria. My parents also helped justify my inability to remember because they reinforced my schoolteachers' allegations that I was a stupid child, who stuttered and was unable to read. At that time, no one was aware of my dyslexia, and I simply surmised that I was too stupid to remember my childhood.

With advancing age, my tucked-away abuse took over even my happiest childhood memories, and I could no longer maintain the façade. Ticking behind the scenes of my repressed childhood was the clock of evolution. When the alarm sounded, my life changed in an instant. Two incidents in 1985, one after the other, awakened my forgotten childhood. First, I separated from my husband; second, my daughter was diagnosed with scoliosis and, as a result, I was introduced to the chiropractic profession.

Since my husband was a physician, and I a registered nurse, we initially consulted the traditional medical profession for our ten-year-old daughter's health. However, when they recommended surgically implanting a metal rod into her back, I began to look for other solutions. In my nursing career, I had seen patients with similar spinal rod surgeries confined to a wheelchair later in life, and I refused this procedure for my daughter. I waited for that solution.

One day a friend introduced me to the chiropractic profession, which surprisingly offered a way to heal without drugs and surgery. Fortunately for my daughter, her scoliosis was in its early stage, and her back straightened with a few adjustments. I too enjoyed some benefits. I had a decrease in the severity of my headaches and perceived an image emerge from the darkness of my mind. The image was me as a child, sitting alone on my bedroom floor, wiping the blood off my bleeding legs from belt-strap whippings. I remembered asking with my medical mind, "How did I see that image and what happened to me as a child?" Eventually, I was able to answer these questions and recall the sexual abuse.

The exuberance of finding my childhood image soon faded with the apprehension of my physical problems, and I drifted into depression once again. I now knew I had several situations that needed attention. I too had scoliosis similar to my daughter and mother. I also knew its devastation. My mother's advancing scoliosis compressed her rib cage to the point that her lungs were unable to expand fully. Her breathing capacity diminished to such a degree that she could only walk short distances and slept upright in a chair. Even though my scoliosis was not as extreme as hers, I was told that manipulative therapies could not help my bent spine.

Furthermore, I had to consider my congenital heart disease. I had a mitral valve deformity and at this time it had advanced into significant mitral valve regurgitation. Some fifty years ago, in the early days of heart surgery, and at the beginning of my career, I was a nurse with an open heart surgical team. I witnessed the surgery's many shortcomings, and I declined it for myself. My father's mitral valve surgery was successful. Over time, his new valve deteriorated, and his age prohibited a replacement. I believed that I made the right decision not to undergo heart surgery, but now my malfunctioning valve weakened the ventricle of my heart and surgery was no longer an option.

I knew everything had a solution, although I had not found the one for me, yet. I loved life, and I wanted to raise my three daughters with love, not the anger of my past. Oh, my three daughters! Their love and beauty gifted me with the preciousness of motherhood. My daughters introduced me to an unexpected experience of childhood wonder. We had fun snow skiing, studying, cooking, and overcoming our disagreements. I proclaimed that I would find a solution.

I remembered in my nursing career the many oppositions I overcame establishing one of the first hospital and home-based, artificial kidney hemodialysis units in 1967 at Thomas Jefferson University Hospital. I also remembered how satisfying it was when we succeeded. We had diverse challenges as we tested creative ways to implement kidney dialysis that was safe, nurturing, and cost-effective. I learned that if I kept my resolve, the solution would eventually appear. I believed the solution was always there, but it was not the right time, or I was not ready for it. Now I had to apply the same resolve to my health.

I attended traditional psychotherapies as a way to address my childhood abuse. The talk therapy sessions helped me make more sense of my life, but guilt and depression still took over. If it were not for motherhood and my love of life, the inevitable tears of confusion, emotional pain, and guilt would have consumed me. I joined other therapy groups, but they also seemed to focus on what had happened instead of how to overcome the nagging pain of unresolved traumas.

One time in a therapy session, I remembered a mystical event in my childhood where I felt a place of sanctuary embraced by love. I did not share the encounter with my therapist because even in 1990, spiritual experiences were considered psychological disorders. For this reason, I abandoned traditional therapy. The following day I again felt my connection to the universe, which gave me a profound love for humanity and a determined spirit. However, my body and mind needed time to adapt to the heightened consciousness of another dimension of reality. My daughters' schedules kept me aware of my needs of eating and sleeping. Soon, I felt revitalized to begin a new chapter.

I started to write how I felt as some therapists suggested, but my dialogue took a different direction. Instead of writing about my feelings I wrote to each emotion as if I was talking to my friend. Clueless of any therapy or writing process, I allowed the focus of my intense feelings take me where they needed to go. I came to understand many things as the intuition of my soul was guiding me on a natural way to heal. I had a set of unconscious emotions within my inner self who could take form as a character that represented my thoughts and experiences. To recover completely, as I desired, I had to address them. As an adult, I could re-parent my abused younger child self within me, through a loving and accepting dialogue. Ironically, the simultaneous separation of myself into both adult and child helped me feel more connected to myself, not less. How simple! I could access my unconscious through my inner emotional self to heal and change my behavior. The simplicity was the answer to my prayers, and it gave me the life I now enjoy.

At first, my writings with my emotions flourished. I felt love and a sense of belonging. In time, I felt resistance as if I had hit a brick wall. I did reach a wall. Today, I realize I unwittingly found SHAME/GUILT. The SHAME/ GUILT that I unconsciously carried was an emotional wall of denial and repression. Denial, which helped me cope in my earlier years, blocked me from feeling and my recovery.

Shame felt like an odd word. I sensed nothing as if I were in a daze. At that moment, I started my SHAME/GUILT mission as I tried to understand shame. After a visit to the library, I could connect shame with my feelings of not being good enough but nothing else. I surely identified with guilt as it haunted me daily.

Reflecting on my childhood and my fifteen years of education in a religious environment, I learned that I was a sinner who should feel shameful, guilty, and needed to repent. My mother said I was bad because I did not exactly do as she did. Since I was bad, I concluded that God punished me with the inability to read. I feared God, so I searched within my mind and heart for my wrongdoings that caused me not to read, but I could not find them. With my child mind, I surmised that I was bad when I thought of doing something wrong.

The SHAME/GUILT of my childhood clung to me like a thirsty leech, but my innate intelligence kept me on the path towards resolution. The resolution came in the most unlikely encounter. Another part of my inner emotional self came forward into my awareness that echoed judgments of "I am not good enough". AHA! I found my inner critic. I soon came to learn the importance of the inner critic. My superego was my inner critic who produced denial and the many judgments I gave myself and also accepted from others. He chanted the guilt that imprisoned me in depression and was, unfortunately, "the real master of [my] personality."[3] I did not want it controlling my life, but my inner critic did. It seemed that my superego wanted to keep me emotionally safe from traumas. At that time, he only knew the false protection of judgments and denial from my culture.

I and my superego had to come to an understanding before I could continue communicating with my emotions. I had to help my inner critic understand how criticisms and judgments stopped me from my healing and career growth. I offered him gratitude for his protection while silently holding him in my awareness as I went about my daily activities, especially before I went to bed and when I awoke. I discovered that my inner critic was an unconscious duplication of my parents, teachers, and other authorities who also protected me with the abusive strategies of my culture. I further explained to him how I could be emotionally safe with the knowledge of abusive behavior not the use of it. Through mutual support, we came to an agreement, and my inner critic gave me permission to resume the communications with my inner self.

My repressed anger and headaches now had a voice. When invited, my anger and sad emotions came forward, as long as I maintained non-judgment. Our short sessions flourished, and I could sense and then eventually visualize children of different ages within my inner self. Each of

---

3   Edmund Bergler, http://en.wikipedia.org/wiki/Edmund_Bergler (accessed 14Oct.2014).

my inner children or emotions had their version of trauma and joy. From that day, I knew that the past, both happy and sad, still lived within me and would continue. It was my responsibility to unite the negative and positive emotions within my inner self. I could change my outer world to success and happiness when I changed my inner world from trauma to peace.

My emotions took me on their journey, and I felt the abuse they carried, which made them angry and sad. My sadness was me, a small child with tangled, golden hair who wore a torn, pink dress. She sat alone in the darkness as tears streamed down her face. I welcomed my sad inner self instead of casting her away. She reminded me of the time that a teacher stood me in front of the class to read while other students laughed at my stuttered voice. I supported her as a mother would comfort her child. I found my sadness to be a beautiful child of love who got lost in shame. I wept with love and began to feel love for myself along with the excitement of a treasure hunt as I searched for other, separated parts of my inner self. I found children of different ages, who sat alone in dark corners, but I could not see the details of their clothing nor did they want to communicate. Soon my headaches began to diminish.

I juxtaposed two pieces of prose I wrote years apart from each other to illustrate the change in my feelings with the healing dialogues with my wounded inner self. Even though I wrote the 'Today' prose in the present, the personality part of my inner self retained the time of their initial trauma.

YESTERDAY

Years ago, I was told to nurture my inner child.
I felt embarrassed when
I heard the concept of the little child within.

I wanted to ignore my inner child.
I wanted to deny I was ever a child.

I am a grown-up, and I am not a little child.
As an adult, I can think away my pain.
I do not want to meet my little child inside me.

TODAY

I scurry into the forest of love to
find the jewels of my childhood.
I look and see and touch the jewels of my heart.
I claim myself.

I see the catatonic child frozen within me.
I feel her lingering defeat.
Bobby socks and vintage skirts
return me to childhood.

She listens to every word hoping I will address her.
I say, "I love you" and the blackness disappears.
She lifts her downcast head and stares into my

When I first became aware of my inner self, I saw myself in darkness so dense I could not penetrate it. I now identify the darkness as the wall of repressed SHAME/GUILT I unconsciously carried. When I released SHAME/ GUILT, the darkness disappeared, and I finally felt self-love. My inner self of children with the inner critic got up from their crouched positions and replaced their dark, shabby clothing with fresh up-to-date colored outfits.

Once I communicated with my inner self and was able to identify and remove SHAME/GUILT, we began to heal. The healings of my inner self became mine as well. To my astonishment, my healed inner children shared their youthful energy and I was able to heal myself. Without my conscious awareness, their youthful energy continued to nourish me throughout the years. One day another emotional child that mirrored my scoliosis came into my thoughts. She presented herself around the same time I discovered an innovative chiropractor who had the ability to realign my back and neck. Both of us began to straighten our posture. I was surprised and ever so grateful that the chiropractor also had the ability to strengthen my heart muscle. I felt energy surge within me as my deformed mitral valve began to repair.

My inner critic offered me the greatest opportunity to evolve. I now could realize the devastation of SHAME/GUILT within my life. It scarred me with a distorted sense of self that submerged me into the darkness of revenge. I saw myself a victim. I also realize how it distorts a parent's love into abusive behavior. I believe my parents could not see another way from their generations of abuse. I came to understand that SHAME/GUILT, similar but opposite to love, remains within our families and us. It proliferates for generations. The healing of my inner self released me from SHAME/GUILT and brought me into love. It dispersed throughout my life and unexpectedly continued to my children and parents. My parents, my daughters, and I spent many happy days together. As an adult, I feel my parents' goodness and love, and I respect their hard work to raise a family in the times of the Great Depression. I cherish the courage and optimism I cultivated in my childhood.

Others noticed how quickly my health improved, and they wanted to do what I was doing. I assumed they could. After all, I spoke to my inner self the same as I would talk with a child. I combined my innate sense of healing with my nursing skills and opened my life to them. They too healed, and their friends and relatives sought my guidance. I helped each person with the same information regardless of their emotional situation. For the past fifteen years and hopefully many more to come, I have been assisting others out of the anguish of SHAME/GUILT while teaching them how to avoid it in their everyday lives.

Through the years, I noticed that most people demonstrate SHAME/GUILT behavior. It is the root of low self-esteem, and it keeps us in the loneliness of fear and despair. Today, the health industry mentions the mental illness epidemic as they cite an increase of people who seem to express low self-esteem, depression, and other emotional disorders.

Sara Bengtsson, a cognitive neuroscientist, devised an experiment that demonstrates what we think about ourselves significantly impacts our behavior. She illustrated how the words we hear change the self-concept we hold in our mind. She used stupid and clever wording to prime the participants within her study and scanned their brains while testing their performance on cognitive tasks.[4]

---

4   Sara L. Bengtsson, Raymond J. Dolan, Richard E. Passingham, "Priming for self-esteem influences the monitoring of one's own performance," *Social Cognitive and Affective Neuroscience*, Oxford University Press (09/01/2011).

Bengtsson found that when the participants received the stupid priming text they had more errors than when primed with clever wording. She explains that the lack of confidence in the participants' memories after stupid priming explains why if you think you are going to do poorly then you probably will. Also, when the participants received the stupid priming, they did not slow down after making an error. In fact, they continued to make more errors and their performance deteriorated over the course of the experiment. In contrast, when the participants received clever wording they expected to do well, and they did.[5]

Several factors have inhibited the study of shame and guilt that increased its power. One, SHAME/GUILT incites pain. Human nature propels an individual to do their best to avoid pain. In fact, our instinctive biology is three times more interested in stopping pain that having pleasure.[6] Another factor is that shame implies a cultural stigma. "The idea that shame is taboo in modern societies, to the extent that it proves to be true, suggests the need for more discussion and studies. If shame is a key to understanding human relationships, we will need to bring [it] out in the open."[7] Fortunately some in the healing professions now openly speak of shame.

---

5   Sara L. Bengtsson, Will D. Penny. "Self-associations influence task-performance through Bayesian inference," *Frontiers in Human Neuroscience* (August2013|Volume7|Article490 |12).

6   Neil Patel, "Try These Three Neromarketing Tips." http://*Inc.com*(Sept.25,2014).

7   Scheff,Thomas, *The S-Word is Taboo: The Shame System in Human Societies*. Norbert Elias Foundation.

It was time to write a book to challenge the present beliefs about SHAME/GUILT that would help anyone regardless of their emotional situation. Words bubbled out of me as if they were alive, but soon SHAME/ GUILT and dyslexia led me to confusion. Nevertheless, with each step out of my SHAME/ GUILT handicap, I grew stronger and wiser to write this book. I offer education that will guide others to counteract its tricky ways. We can win our inner fight of not being good enough or blaming others for our inadequacies. Fortified with knowledge and desire for health, anyone can oust SHAME/GUILT, reclaim their lives, and evolve into greater consciousness.

"Life has spun out of time.

Let it be among all people
to begin their life as the bosom of the earth
and
the love of the tides.

One's heart seeks its freedom
as stated in the treaty of love
established
at the moment of creation.

The music of one's soul
sings its song for its release
and
beckons to be heard.

The likelihood of listening is greater than before.
All souls await
the connection to their heart.
Yet
one's heart cannot be heard
when
SHAME/GUILT
clamps it still."[8]

---

8   Lois Hollis, *Universe Speaks*, (Arizona: Soulspeaks Publishing, 2008). p.19

CHAPTER TWO

EVOLUTION OF CONSCIOUSNESS

"The wonder of our imagination resides in our potential.

We are much, much more
than what
SHAME/GUILT told us."[9]

"Knowledge of, or a belief in, the continuity of life has a tendency to uplift humanity, to make of man a desirable neighbor, a good citizen, a moral upright being and a practical understanding of right and wrong."[10] Evolution is a natural phenomenon. "The ability to rise and go beyond limitation and restraint, is our biological birthright, built into us genetically and blocked by enculturation."[11]

---

9   Lois Hollis
10 Daniel David Palmer, *The Chiropractor* 1914, (Los Angeles: Beacon Light Printing, 1914) 10.
11 Joseph Chilton Pearce, *The Biology of Transcendence*, (Vermont: Inner Traditions, 2004), 225.

Humanity evolves naturally into a higher or greater consciousness; cosmic law dictates evolution, and every aspect of life evolves continuously. We may want to stop the treadmill of self-evolution, but stagnation causes emotional pain within our souls. Socrates's statement, "The only true wisdom is in knowing you know nothing," explains the cosmic dilemma of eternal progression. Nonetheless, the guidance of our immortal soul continues onward.

We have come far and done well to progress beyond former SHAME/GUILT limitations, but a thirst for more still exists! Inspiring authors taught us empowerment and supported our innate creativity. Motivational speakers enlivened us with their messages of positive thoughts, organizational skills, and cutting-edge technology. Other authorities advocated introspection to remove emotional obstacles that blocked our personal and career goals.

SHAME/GUILT RETARDS SELF-EVOLUTION

SHAME/GUILT keeps us in an automatic state of our primitive reptilian brain which usually controls our behavior. "…even when we think we're being rational and conscious, we're largely being driven subconsciously by previous similar experiences and emotions. Psychologists generally agree that at best we are only 15 percent conscious of our motivations and behaviours."[12]

From birth, most of us have an innate sense of right and wrong, and if nurtured, will expand. SHAME/GUILT blocks our connection with our souls that is necessary to feel love and establish compassion, in addition to the development of moral principles. Without its interference, our natural sense of interconnectedness matures and we learn to respect the connection to our fellow man. We will use our energies for self-evolution rather than prejudices and warfare. We trust our innate wisdom that knows what is right and wrong to direct our ethical choices. We will live with the gratitude of our souls, not SHAME/GUILT consequences.

---

12   Dr. Sonja Gwosdezki, http://integratedwellness.com.au/

Evolution is our natural instinct. Evolution quickens our mind and shifts us out of SHAME/GUILT limitation. Self-evolution offers us the opportunity to remove the obstacles in our eternal path. Inside evolution, love and light energies join in agreement with our souls so that we can heal and regain our innate attributes. The light of truth melts the arrogant judgment of pride and unworthiness. Fear dissolves in the banquet of love and the echoes of unworthiness fade. Our nervous system reclaims its energy from SHAME/ GUILT to restore our lightbody. Our soul influences our genetic line as it continues from one lifetime to the next. Each generation may add or reduce its quantity of SHAME/GUILT karma.

The battle ends. SHAME/GUILT is part of being human, but it is also the antithesis of self-love. We are evolving out of the trap of suffering and servitude. It is a toxic outside force, and we peacefully can walk away. Knowledge illuminates its whereabouts and it has no place to hide. Admittedly, we have repressed SHAME/GUILT that lurks within us, but it is not ours to own. We can release the SHAME/GUILT leech, reclaim our energy, and live our authentic sense of abundance and interconnectedness. Without it, we can honor ourselves together with our fellow man. We will share the blessings of heaven and earth within our personal field that empowers our eternal progression. We naturally live within the birthright of our soul that grants us a positive state of being within each moment.

Love and light energies raise its curtain of illusion. The light of knowledge illuminates secrecy, and truth pierces servitude. We can see a glimmer of accountability in the corporate sector. Let us capitalize on this new wave of energy and be detectives to oust its reign of suffering. Focused on our mission, we will not get lost in its games of confusion and hypnosis. Our healed inner emotional self strengthens into harmonious unification and leads us into genius rather than the fragmented personality of mediocrity. This time, we will succeed.

CHAPTER THREE

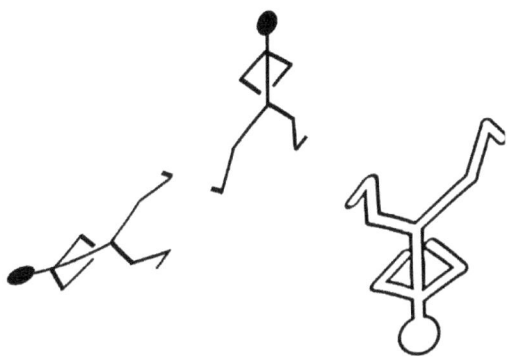

SHAME/GUILT

WHAT DO SHAME AND GUILT MEAN TO YOU?

Innocently, we define shame and guilt through our experiences, the opinions of others, and our culture. Our behavioral choices concerning shame and guilt stem from our definitions. The majority of cultures identify unworthiness and wrongdoings with the words shame and guilt. We perceive guilt as I did something bad and the need to repent. In contrast, we perceive the word shame as I am bad. Throughout the ages, we have amassed many definitions for the origin and meaning of shame and guilt, which abound with biblical, mythological, and spiritual overtones. Eastern and Western cultures, as well as their subcultures, proclaim opposing definitions. SHAME/GUILT can be considered good, bad, healthy, or toxic. No surprise that it can exploit and reinforce its cycle of abuse.

AGAINST SHAME

- "Life is easy for the man who is without shame."[13]
- "Who has no shame all the world is his own."[14]
- "Shame corrodes the very part of us that believes we are capable of change."[15]
- "Shame is a soul-eating emotion."[16]
- "I count him lost, who is lost to shame."[17]
- "We but half express ourselves, and are ashamed of that divine idea which each of us represents."[18]

FOR SHAME

- "The only shame is to have none."[19]
- "He who has done a shameful deed must conceal it, for revealing one disgrace is to commit another disgrace. A concealed shame is two thirds forgiven."[20]
- "Who is not shamed by his sins, sins double."[21]
- "What is no sin, is no shame."[22]
- "Any science or culture that tries to excise guilt from the psyche is creating moral Frankenstein monsters... A person without the ability to experience shame and guilt becomes a sociopath and a psychopath."[23]
- "Men cannot live without shame. A sense of shame is the beginning of integrity."[24]

---

13   Buddha Sutra,*The Dhammapada, Vol 7"* by Osho.
14   Jon R. Stone,*The Routledge Book of World Proverbs,*(NewYork:Routledge,2006), 385.
15   Brene Brown, PhD, https://www.goodreads.com/quotes/383047 accessed 02/22/2013.
16   C.G.Jung,*Red Book.*
17   Titus Maccius Plautus,Bacchides(111,3,80)
18   Ralph Waldo Emerson, *Self-Reliance Essays,*(1847)
19   Blaise Pascal, Pensees
20   Jung Nyun Kim Cho, Muslim-Christian Encounter,127.
21   Jon R. Stone,*The Routledge Book of World Proverbs,*(NewYork:Routledge,2006), 385.
22   Ibid..
23   Kenneth Woodward, "Whatever Happened to Sin,"*Newsweek,*Feb.1995.
24   Mencius Chinese Philosopher,

"The difficulty in studying shame in modern societies is…the s-word is still taboo. For that reason, there are many studies of the shame system, but hidden under other terms: fear of rejection, disrespect, stigma, honor cultures, revenge, etc…Writings that have shame in the title have met particularly strong resistance, both frequent rejection by the editor without circulating to referees, or rejection after circulation…The taboo on shame has many weakening effects on knowledge because it cordons off into separate groups what ought to be a single field, reinforcing the existing taboo. My experience gave me the feeling that shame is a taboo topic for most people, including most researchers."[25]

In most cultures, the word shame scorns our loving heart with the suggestion of a personal deficiency that demands punishment. It activates our repressed SHAME/GUILT as if it were the detonation cord to a bomb. Instantly and unexpectedly, it exposes the secret traumas that we believe have vanished. As we propel towards self-evolution, under no circumstance do we want to hear the word shame and disclose our inadequacies, hidden traumas, and secrets. Most of us are afraid of what shame will tell us and use the mask of denial to block our mistakes, imperfections, and other follies.

SHAME/GUILT has taken us on a wild ride to nowhere, meanwhile wounding our vital life essence. Our unconscious mind stores our repressed SHAME/GUILT where we cannot readily recognize it with our conscious awareness. Some defensively proclaim they have no shame or can protect themselves from emotional hurts. Others may say; "What are you saying? I am good. I volunteer to the sick and donate to the poor. Good people do not have shame."

In a sense, each scenario is correct. Adults with their educated, conscious minds may deny the shame, but their unconscious or inner selves will probably disagree. At times, denial provides us with the opportunity to strengthen our self-esteem before we can contemplate feelings of unworthiness. Our innate wisdom reveals the appropriate time for our minds to unveil its secrets. Until then, our inner critic must provide protective coping skills called self-defenses such as repression; projection, rationalization, and compartmentalization to block our personal introspection.

---

25   Scheff, Thomas, "The Repression of Shame" Norbert Elias Foundation. Posted on December 5, 2013. Accessed (11 May, 2014)

We are not bad for having SHAME/GUILT if we live in a culture that rules with abuse. By comparison, we are not bad for having toxic fumes in our lungs if we live near an outdated factory that discharges those fumes. We can declare the word shame in our healing without reservation and no longer let our handicap control our lives.

THE SHAME/GUILT CYCLE

"Shame and guilt function as a conjoined force. I offer the term SHAME/GUILT."[26]

Shame is our unconscious voice and guilt is our conscious voice. Popular opinion separates shame and guilt. We view them as independent conditions because they have distinct characteristics. Actually, they present different expressions as a result of influencing different parts of the nervous system.

"Shame affects the autonomic, involuntary nervous system. Guilt affects the voluntary nervous system."[27]

When SHAME/GUILT influences the involuntary or unconscious nervous system that controls our heart, lungs, and other organs, we call it shame. Blushing is a visceral response and can explain how shame influences the involuntary or unconscious nervous system. Shame resides deep within our unconscious mind, and we have the challenge to know that it exists. Usually, we only become aware of shame when an abusive event triggers us. When SHAME/GUILT influences the voluntary or conscious nervous system that controls the movement of our muscles and bones, we call it guilt. Guilt, on the other hand, resides in our conscious awareness, and we readily recognize it.

Since shame and guilt influence different parts of the body, they will exhibit different physiological and physical symptoms. Yes, shame and guilt have distinct characteristics, and we feel them as different, but they are synergistic. They have the same source and, therefore, potentiate each other. Both shame and guilt need our equal consideration. Nevertheless, our debate of the differences between shame and guilt can lock us in its perpetual cycle. We focus on deciphering their dissimilarities, which teaches us to think our emotions rather than feel them. Once we understand the cycle of SHAME/GUILT, we can begin to stop their impact on our lives. If we address shame and not guilt, we remain in unworthiness; if we consider guilt without shame, we also remain trapped. Shame adds more guilt to our personality and guilt adds more shame. The majority of people regard guilt as less damaging than shame. I believe, to the contrary, that guilt is equally or even more detrimental. Guilt continues to generate additional shame while masking itself as borderline acceptable behavior.

---

27   Joseph J.Lipari, DC, conversation with author, 20 Nov.2012.

EMOTIONAL DUALITY

**"SHAME/GUILT
influences emotions
and
we feel unworthiness.**[28]

We have the capacity to hate and love and we can be the saint or the sinner. Each of us has a private world of emotional duality using both negative and positive expressions. In fact, we have different names for our less than perfect side. Carl Jung first called our dark side the shadow. Sigmund Freud labeled it the hidden conscious or unconscious part of our mind.

What gives us duality? A deeper reflection into our personality can begin to offer some clues. Each emotion as well has two sides. Betty Ford revealed how our emotions have opposites. Each emotion has a dark side that can be called our shadow self and a corresponding one of light. We can also label our emotions as yin or yang and positive or negative. We have the combination of judgment versus acceptance. The less judgment we use, the more available we are for acceptance. The less depression we hold, the more compassion we can feel. The list is endless.

Today's research tells us that positive aspects of our emotions and thoughts give us health while negative ones give us physical and emotional disorders. A positive outlook is more popular than a negative one. Nevertheless, we are a divine expression. We are good, and we come from love and light aspects of the universe, from God, or another divine source. We do not have to search for the feeling of love. WE ARE LOVE. How can we have a dark side? How do we possess negativity? What is this immorality that lurks within us? We may call it; sin, devil, evil, and monster to name a few. How do we exhibit bad behavior since our emotions are not bad; our thoughts are not bad, and we are not bad? The puzzle continues.

Emotions are misunderstood. Emotions are not our enemies or nemesis. They are not the annoying parts of ourselves that we need to observe, deny or abolish. Nor are they fragmented parts of us. We and our emotions are

---

a gift to each other. We are our emotions, and our emotions are us. We are connected and interrelated. Most importantly, they carry our love energy. They give us wisdom and the expression of our humanness. Each emotion is a personality part that joins to occupy a grand presence within us. They have a place within our soul and form an aspect to our persona. They help us discover our loving goodness. They are always in motion and give us feelings.

Love is the emotion of feelings. Emotions either positive or negative come from love and use love energy for survival. Love provides the energy to feel which activates the lifeforce within every cell of our body. Feeling is life itself. The more love we embody, the more feeling we can experience and the stronger our life force energy. Contrary to popular belief, intense negative emotions require more love energy. For example; depression gives the feeling of unworthiness. At times, unworthiness is so profound that it feels we lost our connection to everyone even God or spirit. This separation is an illusion of our minds. It is impossible for us to separate from love. We, as well as our emotions and thoughts, live in the energy of love energies. Love is our essence.

SHAME/GUILT can give us an explanation for our duality. Similar to our emotions that create a field of feeling, SHAME/GUILT makes its field of energy. However, its energy creates distortions and, therefore, disrupts our emotions and the love we feel. It has the ability to change whatever it contacts. When it interacts with our emotions it distorts or changes their positive aspect to its negative part. Any external substance can change another substance. We can change cold water to hot with heat energy. A virus can distort or alter computer programs, and SHAME/GUILT separates our personality into emotions that conflict. It distorts our thinking and causes distorted statements that are illogical. God told me to kill my parents is such an example. Lying distorts the truth and is another example.

SHAME/GUILT has also given us the erroneous information that emotions are repulsive because it alters or changes their loving voice. If we fear our emotions, we feel the SHAME/GUILT within them. We often conclude that our emotions are scary and painful. Sometimes its influence is so overpowering that it makes us believe that we should avoid our feelings. Emotions controlled by SHAME/GUILT sabotage our physical, mental, and emotional health while emotions without it bring confidence, passion, healthiness, and the light of wisdom. We and our emotions are both victims of SHAME/GUILT.

Fundamentally, it blocks or separates our emotions from each other and from us to form the shadow personality or as we call it the forgotten self. It distorts our self-esteem into unworthiness. It stops us from feeling. Emotional numbness tells us that SHAME/GUILT has taken over our emotions. It competes with the energy of love for space. It covers each emotion and tricks us into lost lonely feelings. We are not lost; it blocks love. Light and love energies give us our creative spark and it blocks our innate creativity. Love makes the light, and it takes the light. It has an inexhaustible supply of energy because it takes our energy. When we feel negativity we often experience fatigue and when we are positive we feel uplifted. Emotions that are locked in its shadow cause pain. We isolate ourselves in a secret emotional world hidden from our soul and spiritual gifts. Eventually, we isolate ourselves from everyone and everything which is often observed in PTSD of veterans.

Love makes us happy and positive. SHAME/GUILT does the opposite. Love with light regenerates. SHAME/GUILT destroys. It competes with love and light for territory. It suppresses, degenerates, and splits our consciousness into healthy and unhealthy aspects. The divine spark of light stimulates our feelings of love and in return love opens the doorway to more light. Each emotion has its light and love that brings our emotions and mind together. The shared light of our emotions and mind maintains our harmony of peace. Light and love also brings humanity together as we share a connection to universal light.

SHAME/GUILT is not part of us. It is not ours to own. **SHAME/ GUILT is an outside force that alters or distorts our emotions and thoughts.** It deludes and tricks us because we believe in its power. It has no power over us. It takes the energy or power from our emotions to mask its illusion of supremacy. The more energy we relinquish to it the deeper it embeds into our personality. Some everyday statements suggest how we transfer it onto each other.

- Do not put that on me.
- Keep that to yourself.
- I do not take that blame.
- That is your stuff.
- I do not let things get to me.
- You take that back.

Even though it is separate from us, it makes its way onto and into us. First, "We live in an atmosphere of shame."[29] It pervades us if our culture uses SHAME/GUILT to control behavior. Second, as victims or scapegoats, we unknowingly accept it from others. Third, we can use judgments to abuse ourselves.

SHAME/GUILT alters our positive emotions into negative ones, and there it hides. Negativity is not a bad emotional state, but a **deep** state that helps balance our personality. Negativity makes us search for our strengths and weaknesses. Trials and errors give us boundaries. Negative feelings deepen our capacity to feel and love. We need both our negative and positive experiences, but **we do not need SHAME/GUILT**. The wisdom of negativity weaves growth experiences into the fabric of our life which often motivates us to resolve our emotional challenges. Negative emotions and thoughts receive the blame for SHAME/GUILT malicious overtones. It can bring anger into hate similar to adding gasoline to a fire. We unknowingly resist the SHAME/ GUILT repressed within us, and this becomes our stress. Negative emotions need our support for expression not the criticism of its trickery. Negativity does not precipitate emotional damage. SHAME/GUILT within negativity can cause emotional catastrophes. The term "Defensive Pessimism,"[30] gives a positive approach to negativity. Without it, we can offset the damages of an adverse situation.

The knowledge that SHAME/GUILT distorts our feelings and thoughts may help us clarify the erroneous allegations against our egos. Some teachings advocate transcending or the abandonment of the ego. Often our egos are called unhealthy or narcissistic. It also influences the ego. It distorts it into narcissism or victimhood, and we declare that egos are unhealthy. Besides, our egos help us value ourselves. A healthy ego or the term healthy narcissism produces the stability of self-esteem to manage the practicalities of life and overcome unworthiness. To the contrary, a SHAME/GUILT ego or narcissism expresses a blend of arrogant authority mixed with victimization. Any attempt to abolish the ego causes the ego to fight with itself. The metaphor, "the dog chasing its tail" explains the futility of trying to abandon the ego.

---

29   George Bernard Shaw, *Man and Superman*. Act One, p.13.

30   Julie K. Norem, *The Power of Power of Negative Thinking*, (Massachusetts: Perseus Books, 2002).

It is an energy force that influences or distorts our emotions and thoughts. It gives us a false impression of our true nature. Today we define it with several words. Some of these are affect, effect, disorder, and syndrome. However, the consensus is that it is an emotion. It has so deeply fused with our emotions that it is a challenge to see it separate. I propose the expression, **pseudo-emotion**. We need our emotions, but we do not need SHAME/ GUILT. We can release it from ourselves without disowning our emotions. We cannot heal it, but we can heal the effects of it.

SHAME/GUILT emptiness and loneliness can propel good people to do bad things. Even though each of us is a divine expression of the universe with the best intentions of heart, we can exhibit caustic and malicious behavior. Often we may wonder why our behavior does not always follow our best intentions. We can unmask the SHAME/GUILT confusion within behavior. We can understand dysfunctional behavior and the horrors in the world. Our peaceful tolerance will dissolve regrets. We do not need to condone immoral behavior but consider resolutions without hatred. SHAME/GUILT is not an excuse for abusive behavior; it is an understanding of our emotional handicap.

**We expose and dismiss SHAME/GUILT
because
it is not a part of humanity.**

**We recover self-esteem with the power of our emotions
and
grow into wisdom without judgment.**

CHAPTER FOUR

WHY WE FEEL WE HAVE NO SHAME

SHAME/GUILT HIDDEN NAMES

> "We can embrace ourselves and others with compassion
> when we approach emotional disorders as
> a response to SHAME/GUILT
> rather than mental illnesses."[31]

The many diagnoses that psychology uses to identify particular behaviors have the tendency to camouflage SHAME/GUILT. Having different names for an object or person is not unusual, though it makes it challenging to identify the object. There are approximately forty-plus names for MSG used in the food supply including yeast extract, hydrolyzed products, and others. SHAME/GUILT has hundreds of names including but not limited to:

---

31   Lois Hollis

Depression	Regret	Jealousy	Anxiety
Sadness	Loneliness	Spitefulness	Remorse
Procrastination	Grief	Defiant	Overachiever
Underachiever	Self-Abuse	Entitlement	Judgmental
Joke Telling	Hopelessness	Suicide	Homicide
Genocide	Pity	Stealing	Panic Attack
Anger	Hatred	Terror	Addictions
Indifference	Suffering	Sarcasm	Worry
Embarrassment	Lying	Deceitful	Codependence
Arrogance	Criminal Behavior	Hostility	One-Upmanship
Self-Righteousness	Shyness	Neglect	Hoarding
Cheating	Narcissism	Accident Prone	Controlling
Ptsd	Helplessness	Grudges	Low Self-Esteem
Eating Disorders	Phobia	Defensiveness	Paranoid
Sexual Dysfunctions	Laughing-Talking Excessively	Volunteering Excessively	Obsessive-Compulsive
Bullying	Moody	Fear	Anti-Social

The following example demonstrates how we can retrace our destructive behavioral patterns back to their SHAME/GUILT origin.

- Marie awoke early to make her well-known lasagna for her son's second-grade end-of-year school party. As a single mother, Marie had little time to attend Tim's extracurricular activities. Moreover, she looked forward to her chance to contribute and show that she too was a good mom. Ready to leave the house, Marie took the lasagna pan out of the oven. Tim bumped into her as he ran to retrieve his teacher's gift from the kitchen table. Marie lost her balance. The large pan landed upside down on the floor. She screamed with anger at her son, and he vanished into his bedroom. They both attended the school party with grief and anger.

Marie was able to relate her unreasonable expectations and judgments to the anger at her son. Marie released the SHAME/ GUILT within herself and took back what she placed upon Tim, and released it as well. She and her son stopped their cycle of abuse and enjoyed a healthier and happier relationship.

SHAME/GUILT IN DISGUISE

SHAME/GUILT portrays itself as both overt and subtle. We can clearly identify physical abuse, but we may not always recognize the subtleties of emotional abuse. SHAME/GUILT subtleties typically blend into normal behavior and strike with a stealthy quickness. Perhaps we may not acknowledge insidious SHAME/GUILT we still feel our reaction to it. Do a test. Watch your expressions and the expressions of those around you when you say the word shame or you use accusations toward yourself or others?

NOTE: The first list contains typical abusive comments that we may often hear from others. The second list has critical comments that we may say to ourselves. This list has larger blocks to illustrate that the SHAME/ GUILT comments in our voice embed deeper into our consciousness than those we hear from others and, therefore, can cause more emotional and physical harm.

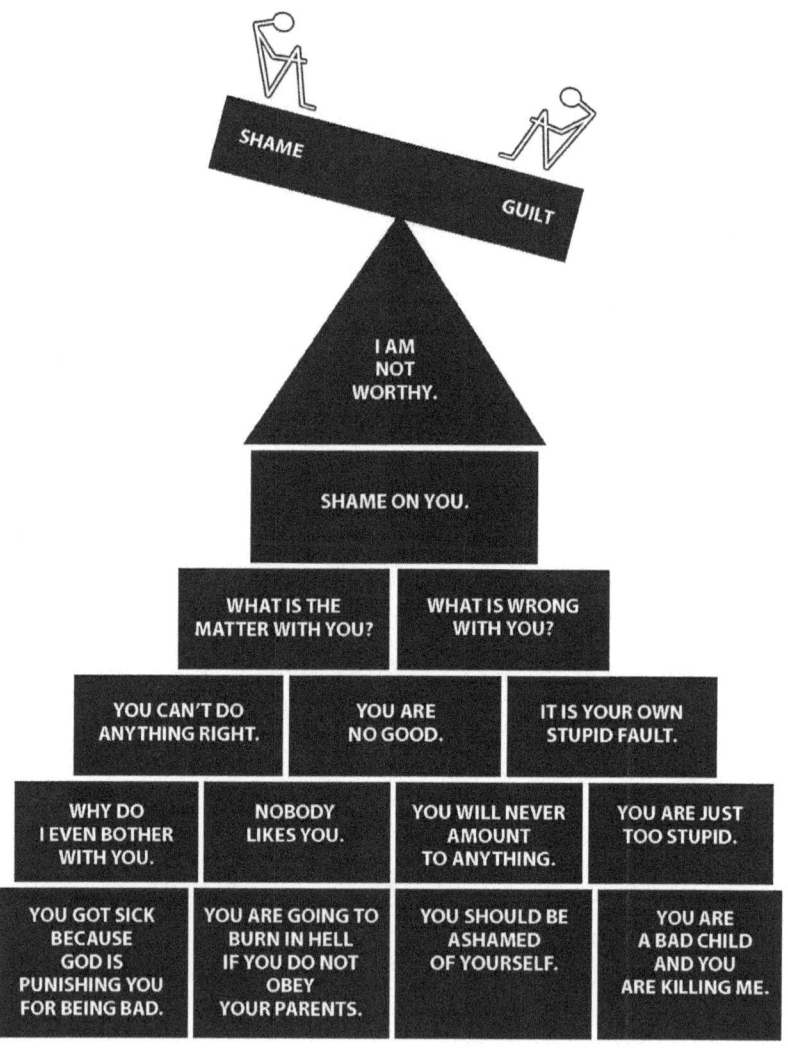

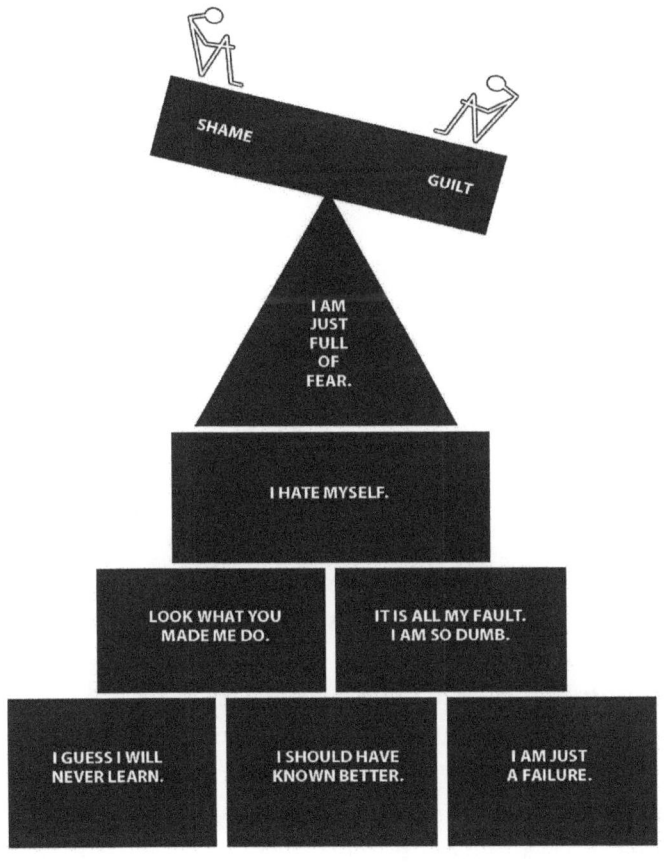

29

MASK OF DENIAL

We may see and hear abusive remarks but consider those comments typical behavior. Repetitious and ubiquitous remarks of SHAME/GUILT create a familiar world of abuse. Its overtones embed in religion, language, education, judicial systems, and consequently within us. We swim in the sea of doubt and unworthiness with critical judgments of self and others. We witness war atrocities and famines. The bombardment of abusive behavior lulls us into its hypnotic submission, similar to the mind's ability to not recognize a low-grade monotonous noise.

To see and feel abuse as normal behavior, we must override our innate sense of moral behavior. We must live in the denial of our innate feelings of love. We achieve our denial with an invisible mask called SHAME/GUILT hypnosis. Our mask of hypnosis instantly compels us to normalize abusive behavior similar to the use of 3D eyeglasses as we view a 3D movie. The movie appears clear if we use 3D glasses, and abusive behavior appears normal when we wear our mask of hypnotic denial. Innocently, it hypnotizes us, and we feel our lives through the distortion of our outer mask and remain in the denial cycle of abuse.

Our inner self of innate knowledge and feeling does not agree with our outer mask of hypnotic denial. What we see is not what we feel. Our mask of denial indoctrinates us to silence our innate sense of moral ethics, and we must construct an inner mask. Early in childhood we begin to create our inner mask of emotional self-defenses that can rationalize or manipulate SHAME/GUILT behavior to seem appropriate and even righteous. We then can justify our mask of hypnotic denial.

Consequently, our mask of denial distorts and stresses our innate sense of right and wrong. We learn not to trust our instincts. We may become writers instead of engineers, doctors or lawyers instead of artists or playwrights; or never find our purpose. In addition, the mask of denial uses our thoughts to cover our feelings and indoctrinate us to think our feelings.

Nevertheless, our evolutionary and insatiable minds still struggle to make sense of abusive behavior and try to understand why it continues. Our minds generate additional SHAME/GUILT for their inability to find a resolution. Our inner mask of denial brings chaos and stress levels of physical and emotional ill health. Some individuals cannot outweigh the heaviness of untruths, and their denied emotions may block their innate sense of love. They may develop a solid wall of arrogant denial or collapse into despair or have a combination of the two.

In SHAME/GUILT cultures, children often receive punishment instead of validation for following their innate sense, which may be contrary to socialized doctrines.

- George, a ten-year-old very sensitive child, was repeatedly beaten by his father. He and his family were devout members of a small community church. From an early age, George had a profound connection to God. He assumed that the priest from his church could help stop the beatings from his father. After school one day, George went to church and told the priest about the beatings from his father. He asked the priest for help because he could not understand why his father beat him. He also begged the priest to keep his visit a secret from his parents. George left the church feeling he would have some resolution to his problem. Unbeknownst to him and against his wishes, the priest contacted George's parents. George endured even more beatings from his father. As an adult, he developed a cynical view of society. Since George believed that priests were God's representatives, he abandoned his belief in God.

  After considerable introspection, George was able to reconnect with his ten-year-old self and re-establish both his adult and childhood self's connection to God. He also removed the SHAME/GUILT from himself and his child self that he took on from his father's beatings and the priest's betrayal.

BELIEFS OF THE SHAME/GUILT MIND

"Truth has no boundaries
once one's heart is open to its love.
The realms of the universe
are ever expanding to encompass the all of ourselves."[32]

Beliefs rule behavior. Our strategic minds store memories to build a belief structure that creates values, which generate feelings to compose the mental computer program that continuously directs our behavior. Without a belief structure, we could not establish an identity. Beliefs dictate decisions on what to do, how to act, and how to feel. If we believe in a spiritual life after death, our belief will comfort us after the loss of a loved one.

Our belief system, most importantly, provides our minds a shelter to survive the ever-changing world, and it can either open or close the door to knowledge. Learning is our mind's most significant asset. Life is not static. All life evolves. Humanity dwells in an evolutionary matrix of expansive knowledge that follows the cosmic law of eternal progression.[33] Sometimes, we take a few detours on the evolutionary road to obtaining extra experiences, but self-evolution never stops. We including our beliefs must change to accommodate new-found possibilities. Healthy minds want to gain knowledge, but minds held in SHAME/GUILT conditioning resist knowledge that opposes established beliefs. Here begins the conflict.

When we receive new information, our minds instinctively compare it with information stored in our memory banks. From this point, we may accept it as valid, discard it entirely, or decide to test its validity. If our minds cannot fit the new information into their belief structure, they usually wait in their comfort zone.

We can contemplate a new belief when we discover why we support certain ideas and untangle our web of SHAME/GUILT misinformation. Without our conscious awareness, our minds archive abusive incidents with our unworthiness memory records. SHAME/GUILT fuses with

---

32   Lois Hollis
33   Daniel David Palmer, *The Chiropractor 1914*, (Los Angeles: Beacon Light
      Printing,1914),10.

what we believe, and we question our self-worth, rather than consider the validity of new information. To even entertain a different belief, we must tackle the SHAME/GUILT influencing our egos, as they say; "I may have been wrong, or I did it the wrong way." We can ask our minds to open to the possibilities of a new belief. Zen teaches to experience everything with a beginner's open mind[34] i.e. without a bias of conditioning prejudices. When we resolve the SHAME/GUILT within our present beliefs, we can consider new information and evolve.

> "Anyone
> who desires to eliminate SHAME/GUILT behavior can
> remove their mask of denial
> open their minds to new information
> identify and release SHAME/GUILT
> regain their innate wisdom and love."[35]

---

34   Shunryu Suzuki, *Zen Mind, Beginner's Mind,* (NewYork:Weatherhill,1999)
35   Lois Hollis

CHAPTER FIVE
CULTURE

> **"Our lives change from fear to compassion
> when we release SHAME/GUILT."**[36]

What is cultural inheritance? Culture is the way of social interactions that orchestrate the moral conduct of behavior; it is neither bad nor good. From birth, the culture programs itself into its people.

TRIBAL SOCIETIES

Some tribal societies such as the Yequana, Senoi, and Aborigines have characteristics contrary to known SHAME/GUILT societies. The Senoi is a group of Aboriginal people living without restraint or law in the remaining Malay jungle. They live recluse to the rest of the world within their ways and belief systems without SHAME/GUILT.

"The Senoi refrained from judging self or others not from some noble virtue but because their minds, not having been formed in the same manner as ours, simply did not function that way—never having been judged or restrained, they had no concept of either and no neural paths for relating in these ways. We, on the on the other hand, having been restrained and judged since birth, automatically judge others, restrain them if possible, and teach our children to do the same."[37]

Jean Liedloff, an American author, and psychotherapist lived two-and-one half years with the Yequana Indians deep in the South American Jungles of Venezuela, and she reported her findings in her book, "The Continuum Concept." She discovered that this tribal culture spent the majority of their time in social groups integrating fun into their chores. They showed each other a sense of innate belonging, which seemed to arise from their soul.

Liedloff observed that the Yequana were some of the happiest people on earth and did not exhibit shame or guilt behavior within themselves or their culture. In fact, their language had no words for shame and guilt, and there is no evidence of it in their culture. Without judgments or accolades, they expressed their identity with their designated work. "Adults [did] not enforce their will upon their child or anyone else." Both adults and children supported each other.

The Yequana adults devoted many resources to their children and carried their infants at all times. The children were allowed to fish and swim without adult supervision at very early ages. Each child developed its innate schedule that naturally followed the schedule of the family and the tribe. Accordingly to Liedloff, the child "is more likely to do what he senses is expected of him than what he is told to do."

Jean Liedloff concluded that since these children were allowed to act with *their innate wisdom,* they developed a healthy self-esteem and sense of responsibility throughout their life.[38]

---

37   Joseph Chilton Pearce, *The Biology of Transcendence,* (Vermont: Inner Traditions, 2004), 257.

38   Jean Liedloff, *The Continuum Concept,* (DaCapo Press: Massachusetts, 1977)

SHAME/GUILT SOCIETIES

"Punishing a man strengthens the culture, which strengthens mediocrity and reduces the human spirit."[39]

Cultures are classified based on shame, guilt, and fear. Intentionally or unintentionally cultures use SHAME/GUILT to secure their agenda and maintain control. The ruling class design laws that dictate how an individual should feel responsible for themselves in relationship to their religion, family, and country. Any culture can rapidly imprint its beliefs onto its people with language, beliefs, and rules which will reinforce a continual cycle of abuse.

JOHN LOCKE

John Locke (1632-1704) certainly was not the only scholar promoting the use of shame to control behavior. Many religious and social orders were and still are active proponents of it. Nonetheless, his teachings helped explain the sanctioning of shame that brought about authoritarian control in diverse cultures. Born in England he was a medical researcher and physician as well as an economist who was considered one of the greatest English philosophers. Locke attended the University of Oxford, and his writings helped develop the political philosophy and platform for our American Founding Fathers. One of his main focuses was how we acquired knowledge. He believed that human beings were born as "blank sheets" without innate or inborn knowledge. He concluded that it was up to society to properly train its people.

In Locke's time, the customary discipline of children was repeated beatings, but the excessive beatings hardened the children and produced even more defiance. Several London aristocrats petitioned John Locke for his discipline recommendations to rear their sons to become gentlemen. In response, he wrote, "Some Thoughts Concerning Education." Initially,

---

39   Joseph Chilton Pearce, *The biology of Transcendence*, (Vermont: Inner Traditions, 2004), 211.

Locke wrote for the upper class, but soon commoners sought his educational principles to raise their status. England and other European countries supported his significant philosophical work on discipline. Locke advocated adding public shaming to the beatings for disobedience; even though he admitted that excessive shaming breaks the spirit of a child. Without any belief in humanity's innate soul abilities, we may understand how he and others could sanction beatings and public shaming. The following are short excerts from Locke's dissertation written in 1693.

§. 55..."Esteem and Disgrace are, of all others, the most powerful incentives to the Mind...If you can once get into Children a love of them the true Principle, which will constantly work...which I look on as the great Secret of Education. §. 56. First, Children (earlier perhaps than we think) are very sensible of Praise and Commendation. They find a Pleasure in being esteemed and valued, especially by their Parents, and those whom they depend on. If, therefore, the Father caress and commend them, when they do well; ... Threats or Blows, which lose their Force when once grown common, and are of no use when Shame does not attend them.... §. 57. ... Children may, as much as possible, be brought to conceive, that those that are commended, and in Esteem, for doing well, will necessarily be beloved and cherished by every Body, and have all other good Things as a Consequence of it. And on the other Side, when any one... falls into Dis-esteem, and cares not to preserve his Credit, he will unavoidably fall under Neglect and Contempt... If by these Means you can come once to shame them out of their Faults, and make them in love with the Pleasure of being well thought on, you may turn them as you please...§. 58... When the Father or Mother looks sowre (sorrow) on the Child, every Body else should put on the same to him, and no Body give him Countenance, till Forgiveness asked... This would teach them Modesty and Shame; §. 59... But when their (parents') displeasure is once declared...restore their Children to their former Grace with some Difficulty; and delay till their Conformity,... §. 48...How obvious is it to observe, that Children come to hate things liked at first, as soon as they come to be whipped…and teased about them; §. 76…have Children never Beaten…for any Fault? This will be to let loose the Reins to all kind of Disorder."…Children should be Beaten; …that the shame of the Whipping, and not the Pain, should be the greatest part of the Punishment. Shame of doing amiss, and deserving Chastisement, is the only true Restraint belonging to Vertue. The Smart of the Rod, if Shame accompanies it not, soon ceases, and is forgotten, and will quickly…lose its Terrour…"[40]

CORPORATION

Neuromarketing is the advertisement and marketing of today. It uses neuroscience or the study of how different parts of the brain respond to words, colors, emotions, and other stimuli that trigger an individual to buy a product. These techniques not only aid businesses to increase sales from an unaware public but they help raise the compliance to public issues such as the prevention of forest fires. Either way they are proven effective strategies to use in any marketing campaign.

SHAME/GUILT makes neuromarketing successful. The seller uses SHAME/GUILT statements that can immediately tag onto the insecurities of prospective buyers. Parents, as well as individuals who want to improve their lives, are especially susceptible to this type of marketing.

Corporations built on these tactics of the culture choose profits over ethics. Some aspiring corporate executives may intentionally flaunt the inadequacies of their competition to push their opponents into failure. One-upmanship is a bullying strategy that includes: diverting, condescending, threatening, and trivializing. Fortunately, today a business trend is developing towards cooperation and partnership both within a corporation and with other companies that increase sales. Consumers likewise are demanding businesses to have ethical practices and holistic products.

---

40   John Locke, *Some Thoughts Concerning Education* (1693), http://books.google.com/ books/reader (accessed 02 Feb.2012.)

EDUCATION

Typically, we remember our favorite school teacher, who gave us support and joy for learning, along with the teacher who diminished us into painful humiliation. The teacher who encouraged us avoided SHAME/GUILT tactics and gave us guidance, even while being disciplined. The same applies today. The quality of education for children seems dependent on the type of school system and the teacher who reflects his personal beliefs on the use of SHAME/GUILT.

The saying, "Children should be seen and not heard" still echoes in the minds of some educators and parents. Today we call it adultism. Adultism imbues SHAME/GUILT and is the antithesis of the culture of the indigenous tribes. It tells children how to feel, rather than support their innate awareness. Adultism tells children that they have no say in their behavior or activities because they are incapable of knowing what is right or wrong. After much criticism of adultism, some adults still use rigid control and find a sense of redemption in fear tactics. In most circumstances, oppression with dominance teaches children to distrust their innate feelings and submit to the agenda of others. In later years, this control often causes adults to have significant emotional disorders such as narcissism, victimhood, anxiety, bullying, anger, and so on. Adultism also intensifies society's SHAME/GUILT behavior with parental abuse to children, and the retaliatory children's abuse toward their parents. Abuse once started in the parental home and the school system, as these two following examples illustrate, can ripple into a child's relationship with themselves and others. They can become judgmental of themselves besides competing with their peers with bullying, jealousy, and thrive on the arrogant selectiveness of gangs and clubs.

- Johnny wanted to keep his prized baseball card collection when his family moved. He was disheartened to leave his friends, but his cards gave him solace. Without notice, his parents discarded his card collection because they needed space in their moving truck. John's parents lacked the parental skills to discuss the baseball card situation with their son beforehand, a discussion that would have validated his feelings. Together they could have reached a solution to trading a toy for his cards or leave his cards with a trusted friend to pick up later. Instead, after the move their teary-eyed son looked ceaselessly to find his card collection. His greatest fear came true. He no longer had his cards. Johnny's parents replied, "Why do you want such a silly thing like a baseball card collection. Get over it and grow up." Johnny's parents tried to escape their feelings of guilt and instead put their SHAME/GUILT on him. Johnny's parents continued their lack of emotional support in other areas of his life. Johnny learned not to value his feelings or himself, and he internalized the SHAME/GUILT as I am bad and became a victim as others took advantage of him.

- Peter, who is nine years old, has a conversation with his parents. "Peter, you know how much your grandparents love you. Now I am not forcing you to visit them tomorrow with us but they miss you and feel so much better after they see you." Statements of this nature tend to make a child feel responsible for the happiness of others.

Today, adultism still pervades the school system. "As of 2012, 19 states authorize corporal punishment in their schools."[41] Parental abuse also persists. Some groups of people beat their children every day because "Beating the Devil out of Them"[42] is the custom. Admittedly, there are those children who require a structured way of life, but today many educators and parents help these children with positive youth development strategies. They may offer motivators, negotiations, boundaries, consequences, in addition to groups that nurture the innate sense of interconnectedness. Some sensitive educators and parents recognize the need for the reassurance of praise to offset the doubts and fear damages of SHAME/GUILT. Nevertheless, required testing and academic placement still challenges teachers to reduce it in education.

A subtle form of SHAME/GUILT teaching happens when a teacher announces the mistakes of his students and uses those mistakes to teach his class. Often these teachers teach their students with incomplete instructions or references. Consequently, students cannot accurately complete their homework assignments and return to the classroom with assured mistakes.

---

41   Gundersen National Child Protection Training Center
42   Murray A. Straus, *Beating the Devil Out of Them: Corporal Punishment in American Families and Its Effects on Children* (New Jersey: Transaction Publishers, 2001)

GOVERNMENT

SHAME/GUILT occupies space because it is a substance even though it is seemingly invisible. It blocks one matter from the other, or it separates anything from its attachment. Any organization that governs with these strategies can separate individual departments from each other and separate individuals within the same department. Each department or person will operate in isolation and deliver information not knowing what their other departments report. The expression, "the left hand does not know what the right hand is doing" explains this approach. An organization of scattered non-communicative parts disseminates conflicting information to their consumers that leads to misinformation, incompetence, and irresolution. Some government agencies and other businesses use the SHAME/GUILT design to displace blame onto consumers instead of accepting responsibility. In these cases, the company easily tags its shortcomings as guilt onto an unaware consumer. Sometimes a company gives the consumer incomplete information. Once again the consumer receives blame for their ignorance of company policies instead of the business taking responsibility. Governments and corporations built on SHAME/GUILT will increase their sales but only in the short term.

JUDICIAL SYSTEM

SHAME/GUILT escalates illegal behavior rather than decreases it. Throughout history and as a result of these misunderstandings the judicial system often sanctions abusive ways to deter crime.

Currently, some desire to return outdated public punishments for minor offenses to the American judicial system. These judicial courts mandate the offenders to carry posters or badges in a crowded place to publicize their crimes. Public humiliation may deter illegal behavior. Unfortunately, it can break the human spirit of the offender and keep the spectators plus the victims trapped in the abuse cycle of SHAME/GUILT anger and revenge.

> "Restraint creates the necessity for restraint, and as it is
> increased, more is needed…Without law there is no sense
> of guilt or shame. But were there no guilt and shame, law
> and restraint would never have been conceived because they

would not have been needed. A human nurtured instead of shamed and loved instead of driven by fear develops a different brain and therefore a different mind—he will not act against the well-being of another, nor against his larger body, the living earth. As a child we know we are an integral part of the continuum of all things..."[43]

Fortunately, the rules are changing within the judicial system. Some innovative people established the restorative justice program that encouraged children and teenagers to make meaningful amends for their transgressions. These progressive programs can help young adults return to their innate sense of compassion.

RELIGION

Many religions offer us consolation in our sorrow and a sense of community. However, some religious officials have unknowingly or knowingly, implored SHAME/GUILT tactics for submission. In their defense, they too have been trained with generations of abuse, but they indoctrinate their congregations to believe that they are righteous. Many people dialogue today within open groups to eliminate such damaging words as sinner and suffering. Still some religious authorities tell their congregations that they do not love God enough, or do the will of God, and they need penance for their salvation. These statements damage not empower as they scar our inner self with unworthiness.

SPIRITUALITY

The New Age movement forecasts the coming of a time that advocates individuals to live a spiritual life with the divine purpose of their soul. Some within this movement also declare that if they desire an untroubled life, they must remain positive and never speak negative words or think negative thoughts. Yet, the continual positive state limits the exploration of

---

43   Joseph Chilton Pearce, *The Biology of Transcendence*, (Inner Traditions: Vermont, 2004), 261.

life's experiences and dismisses the need to learn and evolve. The following story tells how "Just Be Positive" can be a SHAME/GUILT encounter.

- Sandy and Joyce met for lunch. Sandy, overwhelmed with her current problems confided in her friend Joyce. Joyce responded, "Stop being so negative. No wonder nothing works for you. You need to be positive and just forget the past." Sandy felt crushed and had no response. Joyce shamed her for having problems, and she also stated an erroneous statement. We are a composite of our physical, mental, emotional, and spiritual bodies or fields and any force that influences one body will impact the others. Joyce's statement shows that she does not understand that repressed SHAME/GUILT in the emotional system can outweigh positive mental affirmations. Sandy discovered Joyce is an unsafe person with whom to share her feelings.

"We are evolutionary beings, not sinful beings.
Only beauty arises from our souls.

There is no need of suffering.

Suffering crushes the self into separation.
The reward is not there and the hope of tomorrow
will only bring the same.

The temptation is to get love from suffered parts
yet
it is too late to pursue that way.

The seeking of suffering abounds with many
but
the quest of the suffering
suffocates the heart to its true love."[44]

---

44   Lois Hollis

PART TWO

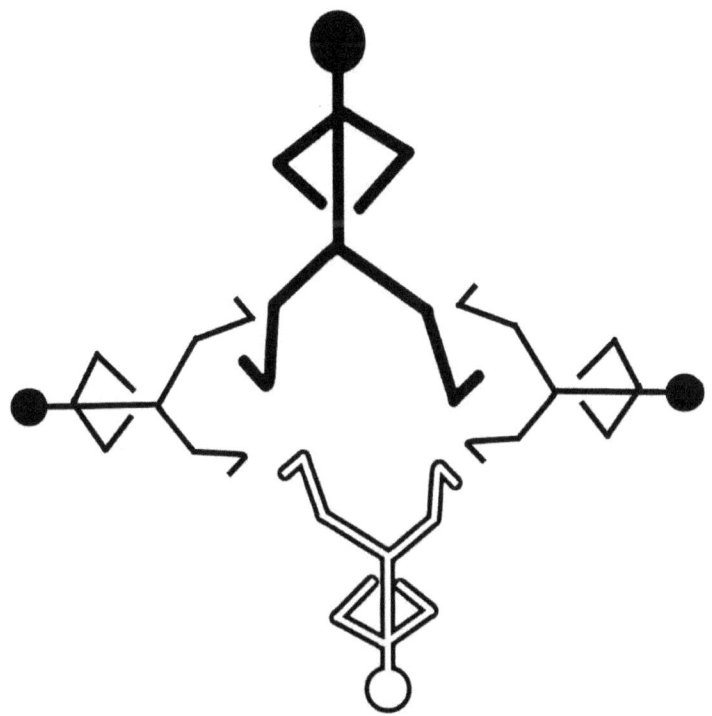

SHAME /GUILT BEHAVIOR

CHAPTER SIX

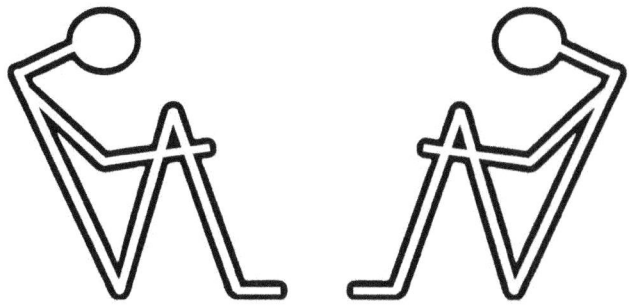

RELATIONSHIPS

"SHAME/GUILT is the primary abuser
in our relationships
with ourselves and others."[45]

What makes us feel good or bad in a relationship? Why do people respond differently to the same information? Why do relationships end even with our best intentions? Relationships are as varied as our diverse behaviors. We have private and public ones but the relationship with ourselves is the most important. Relationships are not a game of chance. They are a game of SHAME/GUILT and can undermine the conversations that shape our relationships.

---

45   Lois Hollis

THE INTERPERSONAL BOND

Our interpersonal bond within ourselves is the best defense against SHAME/GUILT.[46]

Psychology uses the term "interpersonal bridge"[47] to describe the emotional bond of infants or young children to their parents, especially the mother, and any other person who profoundly impacts their life. The closer or more intimate the relationship, the deeper and meaningful the bond. The interpersonal bridge or bond originates in utero with significant persons and continues to strengthen or weaken over time.

Every relationship can establish a healthy or unhealthy bond, but typically it is a combination. The amount of SHAME/GUILT versus love within each partner determines the health of the bond. When the abuse of SHAME/ GUILT enters a relationship, the bond can break and turn from love to mistrust. The interpersonal bond of the abused will most likely break if they experience prolonged, extreme, trauma or the abuser is a family member or trusted friend. The breaking of the bond provides SHAME/GUILT the opportunity to conquer both the shamer and the shamed as each of them detaches from their bond of love to connect with SHAME/GUILT.

Childhood abuse breaks the interpersonal bond early in life. Abuse tells a child that he is bad. The abused child believes he is flawed and unworthy. He hides his innate essence and later in life he may have the challenge to access his core identity. As Joseph Chilton Pearce states, "Shamed in this sense we forget who we are...Cut off from our spirit, we spend the rest of our life trying to prove our innocence."[48] Without full access to his healthy self, he may lose his self-identity and no longer have the trust in anyone, including himself. An abused child frequently develops into a revengeful teenager who returns his vengeance onto his abusers, himself, and others.

---

46   LoisHollis
47   Gershen Kaufman, PhD, *Shame The Power of Caring*: (Vermont: Schenkman Books,Inc.,1992)
48   Joseph Chilton Pearce, *The biology of Transcendence*, (Vermont: Inner Traditions, 2004), 149.

The interpersonal bond is significant to our humanity. Without a connection to ourselves, others or our spirit, we live isolated in the darkness of SHAME/GUILT or PTSD. The sooner an abused child or adult releases it, the less emotional damage follows. Abusers and the abused usually cannot confront each other. In these circumstances, anyone with loving support can validate the victims' painful stories and help them repair their broken interpersonal bond. With love, trust, and the release of SHAME/GUILT, victims of abuse restore their interpersonal bond into love.

INCOMPLETE FORGIVENESS

> "The heart of love or self-love naturally eliminates the need for forgiveness."[49]

The majority of us have forgiven or forgotten those who wronged us. If we re-experience episodes of anxiety or anger, our forgiveness may not be complete. The scar of trauma continues its negativity. The repressed SHAME/GUILT of unspoken anger will readily tag onto present experiences and cause conflicts within our relationships. Forgiveness requires that we take responsibility for our behavior and not continue the cycle of blame. Judgment will add more abuse. Forgiveness completes itself or becomes unnecessary when the abused part of ourselves releases the SHAME/GUILT from their abuser, and we restore our interpersonal bond with self-love.

JUDGMENT

> "Creation begins with the acceptance of self.
>
> Self-love bathes the soul
> in accepting delight
> to remove the
> crusted judgment from a shamed heart."[50]

---

49   Lois Hollis
50   Lois Hollis, *Universe Speaks,* (Arizona: Soulspeaks Publishing, 2008).

Judgment is abuse; guidance, advice, and teaching are not. Judgment is the response or defense of unfulfilled desires. SHAME/GUILT causes a sensory distortion within our emotional body which predisposes the psyche to judgment. When there is no SHAME/GUILT, there is no judgment and the interpersonal bond remains intact. Even though it seems illogical to use judgmental abuse especially upon ourselves, our handicap indoctrinates us to dismiss our innate rights and instead follow its instructions of abuse.

JUDGMENT:

- is the most prevalent abuse.
- infiltrates every area of life and every aspect of ourselves.
- is habitual and addictive.
- reveals the size of our SHAME/GUILT repression or handicap.
- suppresses the spirit of our dreams.
- restricts wonder and creativity.
- keeps our mind in hypnosis.
- develops into hatred if unresolved.
- creates jealousy and remorse.
- shifts our life force away from our soul.
- denies our innate truth.
- occupies our mind with SHAME/GUILT scenarios that lessen our mental capacity for learning and achieving our dreams.

JUDGMENT EXAMPLES:

- "She is such a terrible basketball player. Why does she even play?"
- "I would never do a thing like that."
- "Her clothes never match."
- "Why did I do that? I was so stupid."
- "Why can't I be organized like Judith?"
- "Why can't I stop thinking about it? I should know better."
- "If only I had invested in that company, I would be rich."
- "If only I went to the party."
- "If only I did not go to the party."

"The fluidity of
love
echoes
itself inside the
kingdom of self for
its existence.

The problem of
mankind is that it does not
seek its innate self
but
this is why
man came to earth.

This
remembrance
is the
core
of
humanity."[51]

---

51   Lois Hollis, *Universe Speaks,* (Arizona: Soulspeaks Publishing, 2008). p. 179.

CHAPTER SEVEN

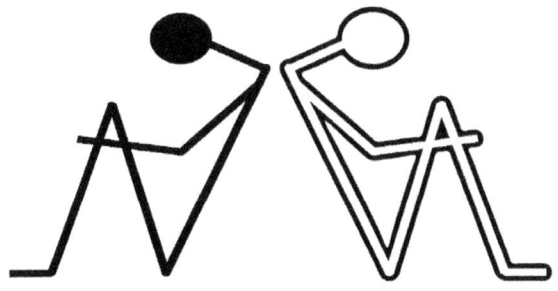

SHAME/GUILT GAMES

"We can feel compassion for ourselves and others as we navigate the imbalance of our narcissism and victimhood tendencies."[52]

Any relationship with self or others receives an invitation to participate in the very popular SHAME/GUILT GAMES. The game requires someone to impose SHAME/GUILT and someone to accept it. The game has either safe or unsafe players. However the majority of people blend into both categories while only a few remain in the extreme. A safe player allows the expression of feelings, speaking from the heart with no ulterior motives, and an unsafe player has ulterior motives. Unsafe players further divide into two categories: the narcissist who is the shamer and the victim who is the shamed. The SHAME/GUILT of each player or between the inner critic and one's self escalates the game. The narcissist challenges its victim much the same as an animal goes after its prey or an inner critic attacks the personal self. The victim unknowingly volunteers to take on the SHAME/GUILT from the shamer. The co-dependence of the victim provokes the narcissist into greater opposition, and the victim escalates his defensive retaliation. At any time, a player may change persona to win the game. A

---

52   Lois Hollis

narcissist may revert to victim persona, or the victim escalates to narcissist persona. The diverse combinations of narcissism and victimhood tendencies woven into daily behavior will provide an exhaustive supply of ammunition for the games.

NARCISSIST VERSUS VICTIM

SHAME/GUILT separates our personality into narcissist and victim personas if we live in a SHAME/GUILT culture. These different personas create a paradox of feeling and thinking; feelings overwhelm victims and thoughts overwhelm narcissists. Narcissists have more narcissism than victim tendencies and those labeled victims have more victim than narcissistic tendencies. We nevertheless have a combination of the two, and under stress, our minds shift from one to the other. A pathological condition exists when we exhibit constant narcissistic or victim behaviors.

Narcissists defame their victims to win the argument. Victims use excuses to receive accolades. Narcissists tend to spark the match, but the victims sustain the fire with relentless unworthiness. Both personas live in their private world and are incapable of understanding the viewpoint of the other. Judgments and criticisms boomerang and intensify the game. Similar to a runaway train, no logic stops righteous narcissists or victims. Once a game reaches a stalemate, the opponents generate additional SHAME/GUILT for their personal deficiencies to win. They both struggle for acknowledgment, underneath the shadow of SHAME/GUILT.

Most people tend to dislike narcissists and feel sorry for victims, even though, both can instigate the game. Labeling individuals narcissistic excites them into anger. In contrast, victims usually feel reassurance when called a victim. Resolution depends on the quantity of repressed SHAME/GUILT within the players. SHAME/GUILT maintains control until one player ends the game either with exasperation or the graciousness of unemotional statements. Narcissists may ask for redemption with such comments as; "Oh I was just teasing you." Players may feel themselves the winner if they had the last word, but the winner allows his opponent to have the last word. In the end, the winner is the player who refuses to play.

NARCISSIST
THINKING PART

Narcissism is the SHAME/GUILT distortion of our natural longing and self-evolution towards perfection. It alters our evolutionary instinct into the need for control and importance. It benefits the corporate world but dictates unreasonable higher standards and responsibilities. Attention to detail and perfectionism serve the narcissist. Nevertheless, the distorted self-importance demands unnecessary responsibility that the world exploits.

Control dominates narcissists and surprises are unacceptable. They believe they control their life, but SHAME/GUILT controls their mind with low self-esteem and unworthiness. The perfectionistic or SHAME/GUILT egos of narcissists record the faults of others. Their mental records supply them with defaming information to sabotage others at their most vulnerable moment. Narcissists conceal their mistakes especially if it uncovers a secret flaw as their inner critic punishes them for any error.

The SHAME/GUILT of narcissists paralyzes their emotions into silence, and they think more than they feel. Their inability to feel stops them from validating others for their display of feelings. They have a difficult time to feel compassion, as the following example, suggests. "Look what you did to my car! It has a huge dent." As opposed to, "Are you hurt?"

Narcissists' fleeting sense of power is the arrogance of SHAME/GUILT. Self-absorbed drama helps them retain dominance as others submit to their agenda. They win their competition as they announce grander successes and failures. Narcissists compliment themselves instead of others with the following statement. "Congratulations on your new job. I am glad I put in a good word for you." Confusion is one of their traits to maintain control. Often they may use uncommon words to continue the confusion and declare their superiority. Narcissists usually hide their code of behavior until someone breaks it, at which time the rule-breaker receives intimidation. When others finally know the rules of the narcissists, they change them. They feel that others should automatically know everything about them as this example demonstrates.

- Samantha wants to buy her friend Carla a birthday present. Samantha is aware of Carla's particular choices and asks her what she would like for a present. Carla states that she is not picky and would like anything that she buys. Samantha shops with great care and finds a scarf that she feels Carla would appreciate. When she presents her well-chosen gift, Carla states, "Oh my, I detest wearing scarfs especially the color yellow. How could you not know that about me?"

Lastly,

narcissists usually manipulate conversations to have the last word.

VICTIM
FEELING PART

Victims oppose narcissists but equally exploit control as they use SHAME/ GUILT to be their caregiver. Co-dependent, enabler, passive-aggressive, and "I want someone to love me and take care of me" describes victims. Victims attend to others' needs and dismiss their own but may secretly hold resentments. Victims are as crafty as narcissists. They demand attention but parade with the drama of hopelessness to win their agenda. Unlike narcissists, victims utilize defensive behavior to hide their secrets of resentment and anger. Victims may sulk in procrastination and confuse any situation by saying and doing the opposite.

Victims usually have a distortive perception of loyalty. They often obey orders, even if they are contrary to their beliefs while defending their abuser with excuses. In this way, victims justify their suffering and delay their emotional recovery. As opposed to narcissists, victims exaggerate their emotions. They defensively overreact to judgments and fall into abandonment with delusionary, low self-esteem. Indulgent to their no-hope scenarios, they listen to SHAME/GUILT and believe that their unworthiness is too big to resolve.

PROTECTION RULES

GIVE NO SHAME/GUILT
ACCEPT NO SHAME/GUILT[53]

Knowledge of the games helps to improve the effectiveness of our conversations. We can have more effective, clearer, and enjoyable communications. We can emerge from emotional isolation to experience more of the world while we remain safer from emotional abuse. Not only can we have a greater circle of friends but we graciously appreciate present ones. Keep alert for abusive statements. With practice, we no longer throw the daggers of insults or accept them. We have a better understanding of behavior to adapt our responses and not build emotional walls that limit friendships. Of course, we are not impervious to emotional insults within conflict. Off guard others can pull us back in encounters but we can view the experience as part of the game rather than a personal attack. With our keen sense of deduction we can acknowledge our contribution to the game as we continue to clarify behavior from the SHAME/GUILT handicap.

STATEMENTS TO AVOID

- "I am sorry, but I really did try. I did the best I could do."
- "I guess I am no good."
- "That was stupid!"

SITUATIONS TO AVOID

- sharing personal feelings with unsafe people.
- the opportunity to tease, play or entice others.
- trying to please a narcissist.
- giving advice unless directly asked.
- confusion and judging.
- excessive and unnecessary explaining.

---

53   Lois Hollis

NEUTRAL REPLIES

Although these rules can provide a sense of confidence in conversations, SHAME/GUILT can still blindside us. Typically, abusive statements happen quickly without adequate time to formulate a response. Time and practice will arm us with an arsenal of neutral answers to stop the game before it begins. Look for truth, accept responsibility, take what is valuable, and discard the rest. **Under no circumstances is it ever appropriate to accept SHAME/GUILT from yourself or others.**

These following neutral remarks can cool the blazing fire of an encounter with SHAME/GUILT and stop the game.

- "That is an interesting approach."
- "That is interesting."
- "You are very creative."
- "Can you say that another way?"
- "You have an interesting point of view."
- "I have to leave now."
- "What are you saying?"

SHAME/GUILT EXPERIENCES

"Our diverse reactions to SHAME/GUILT behavior do not invalidate its existence but support its trickery."[54]

BULLYING

Bullying is a SHAME/GUILT attack upon an individual or a group of people. A bully judges and criticizes a person for having a physical handicap, emotional failing, or a perceived flaw. Bullying can produce more emotional damage than other types of abuse. Victims receive an extensive quantity of SHAME/GUILT from three situations. First, the

---

54

bully attacks the core identity of its victim. Second, a bully often attacks in public and third; the victim may have a relationship with the bully or the witnesses of the attack.

Replacing an abusive statement with a neutral statement will make all the difference in outcomes. Imagine during a gasoline shortage, an affluent community coming together for their annual meeting.

- SHAME/GUILT STATEMENT: The president opens his meeting saying, "I did not see anyone riding a bike to the meeting today." Immediately his words isolate the group. After the meeting few, if any, people gather to discuss ways to address the fuel crisis.

- NEUTRAL STATEMENT: The president opens the meeting saying, "Today we find ourselves in a gasoline shortage. Many factors brought us to this point, but we are a resourceful group. We are organizing an on-going monthly meeting the first Friday of the month at 7 p.m., beginning this week, to find ways to conserve our resources. I look forward to seeing you."

EMOTIONAL NEGLECT

Emotional neglect is the feeling of hollowness and its emptiness is difficult to describe. Neglect illustrates a subtle form of bullying where the abuser is absent. Victims of neglect have no one to blame for their abuse. By default they can only blame themselves and perceive themselves as flawed. They find it difficult to form an interpersonal bond with a significant other and in its place bond with SHAME/GUILT loneliness. Self-condemnation eventually creates emptiness in the soul that never seems to fill. Nevertheless, I have witnessed a recovery in some clients when they address SHAME/GUILT as their abuser.

- Jimmy's father accidentally smashes his six-year-old son's finger as he closes the car door. He screams "Daddy, you hurt my finger!" Jimmy's dad tries to allay his SHAME/GUILT. "Jimmy, your finger is fine, and it does not hurt. I only see a little bruising." Jimmy's finger is bleeding, smashed, and it does hurt. Jimmy will learn not to trust his feelings if his parents continue to invalidate them.

- Bobby is riding his two-wheel bike that he received from his parents for his tenth birthday, but his attention is on the scenery not what is in front of him. He crashes into a large tree and slides under his bike onto the concrete pavement. Bobby cries while holding his painful, bloody knee that peeks through his torn jeans. Immediately his mother runs to his rescue and says "Oh, Bobby! What a mess you made! I was saving those jeans for school." Bobby runs into the house and falls on his bed enveloped with the lonely tears of confusion. He secretly tries to understand what is wrong with him.

PASSIVE-AGGRESSIVE

Passive-aggressive behavior is very common. Individuals who use passiveaggressive behavior display SHAME/GUILT indirectly in contrast to the overt abuse of screaming and beating. They use unclear language to keep their victims stuck in the inertia of confusion. They seem detached from their feelings but usually express them in private. They may not lie, but they manipulate the truth with a defensive attitude. The SHAME/GUILT of low self-esteem does not allow passive-aggressive individuals to ask directly for what they want. Instead, they assume others will somehow know how to fulfill their needs and when they do not, they retaliate with anger. In conclusion, the passive-aggressive person holds themselves to unrealistic goals that turn into critical judgments when they fail.

- Every week Alex tells his wife, Julie another excuse for, not washing his clothes. Either he worked overtime or had extra work at home. He continues to tell her that he will wash his clothes but whenever she approaches the subject; he responds with defensive excuses. Alex does not want to wash his clothes, whether he has the time or not, but he is ashamed to admit it to his wife. The tension between them would dissipate if Alex told Julie his truth, and they could plan accordingly.

- Diane and Tom are having a casual conversation. Diane says to Tom, "By the way, I made a pot of vegetable soup." Tom sarcastically replies, "You cooking again. I am trying to lose weight?" Diane has no response but feels defeated for attempting to maintain nutritious meals for her family. Tom directs his SHAME/GUILT unworthiness onto his wife instead of acknowledging his eating binges.

ENTITLEMENT

We are not entitled to stop traffic as we meander rudely across the street against the light, but we are entitled to a college diploma after completing the necessary courses. Entitlement covers a broad range of behaviors. Any age group displays the immaturity of entitlement, but teenagers seem the most susceptible. They often have to push through the SHAME/GUILT of their childhood to find their authentic self.

SHAME/GUILT entitlement tells us that we do not have to obey the rules because we are more important than other people. Due to the limitations imposed by SHAME/GUILT, we may compensate for our unworthiness with arrogance and elevate ourselves above our fellow man. Arrogance often pushes us into disrespect for ourselves and others. Since we rationalize our importance, we are unable to show compassion. The custom of slavery and oppression is the cruelest examples of entitlement. Sometimes entitlement tells us that we have an important job and deserve special treatment or receive services for free. Customarily religions have a tendency to give their congregations entitlement as they indoctrinate them into the belief that their religion is the best and only one. The inflated importance of some religious sects leads to judgment and eventually wars. Entitlement can also supply our arrogant selves with denial to block the insight into our dysfunctions and say that we do not need emotional introspection.

JUSTIFICATION

SHAME/GUILT is at the core of justification and defensive behavior; it triggers us to use excessive explanations and excuses. A simple statement of fact does not invite nor generate it.

- SHAME/GUILT statement: "Why did you give him money? That was a stupid thing to do."
- SHAME/GUILT REPLY in a victim tone: "I did not know that it would cause a problem. I never would intentionally hurt anyone. I guess I should not have given him the money."
- NEUTRAL REPLY: "It seemed the right thing to do at the time."
- SHAME/GUILT statement: "How could you send your husband to a nursing home? I thought the two of you had a good marriage."
- SHAME/GUILT REPLY: "I really feel awful, but I just could not care for him at home anymore. I am so tired and feel so guilty. My husband deserves more from me, but I am not able to give him the help he needs."
- NEUTRAL REPLY: "We do have an excellent marriage."

SELF-ABUSE

- Alice's computer crashed, and her friend Suzanne recommended Paul, her technician. She told her that Paul is the best. She added that he was expensive and said, "But you get what you pay for." Paul told Alice that her computer was out of date and that he did not repair older models. He would buy her a new one and program it for her.

  Alice would strain her finances if she bought another computer. She told Paul that she would think about it but probably would still go ahead with a new computer. Still uncertain, she asked John another friend to help. John told her that he uses the same computer model and within half an hour, he repaired her computer for a minimal charge. Alice informed Paul that her computer was working and did not need his services. Paul said that he already purchased a new computer for her. Alice re-stated that her computer is in working condition, and she did not need a new one. Finally, Paul agreed to return the newly purchased computer. Without further explanation, she thanked him for his time. Alice realized that she initially felt embarrassed to say that she could not afford a new computer, and it stopped her from being honest about her finances.

TEASING AND JOKING

I consider jokes or teasing a cloaked excuse that an abuser uses to camouflage the abuse he gives to his victims. The statement, "I am just playing with you or making a joke." usually signals SHAME/GUILT and the insulting laughter harms. Publically, the teaser or jokester attacks the core identity or character of its individual victims or social groups with sarcastic statements. A child, as well as an adult, often bears these scar from a jealous abuser. The sarcastic overtones that often accompany teasing or joke telling convey an added dose of abuse.

- Bernadette, a very social and attractive individual, wanted to keep in touch with her newly found friends that she made on her week-long trip. The day before the end of the trip and the return home, she mentioned to David, the trip's leader that she wanted to keep in touch with her new friends. She suggested that he pass a paper around so that those interested could have the opportunity to exchange contact information. David responded in a sarcastic tone: "Why would anyone want to keep in touch with you?" Surprised and overpowered, Bernadette did not answer but quietly collected her new friends' contact information.

SHAME/GUILT SUBTLETIES

The subtleties of SHAME/GUILT come in many ways that make it a challenge to recognize.
- SHAME/GUILT SITUATION:

Anita and Theresa are friends, and they work in the same company. Anita works in computer technology, and Theresa manages sales. Theresa often asks Anita questions regarding her new program she purchased for her computer. Anita does not have time during work hours to help Theresa, so she invited Anita on the weekend to her home. Theresa arrived at Anita's home on time, but Anita seemed agitated. She said, "Oh I should have asked you to come next weekend because I have to take my son Timmy to a birthday party and also pick him up." Theresa felt awkward during the time they did have together, and she did not learn enough to use the program.

- NEUTRAL SITUATION:
  Anita could have a different approach. "Theresa thanks very much for coming, but I made a mistake with my time. I did not realize that I had to take my son Timmy to and from a birthday party. I would like to propose a solution. We can talk while I am driving, and I can show you how to use the program on my computer when we arrive back home."

Anita criticized herself with judgment for forgetting her responsibility of taking her son to the party. Anita's judgments spread onto Theresa, and it stopped them from having an enjoyable day. Most of us live in a fast-paced society, and unforeseen situations sooner or later happen. Anita, without judgments could acknowledge that her plans changed and re-negotiate another plan with Theresa.

> **"If you alone begin to eradicate SHAME/GUILT behavior
> you have given yourself as well as others
> the greatest of gifts!"**[55]

---

55   Lois Hollis

CHAPTER EIGHT

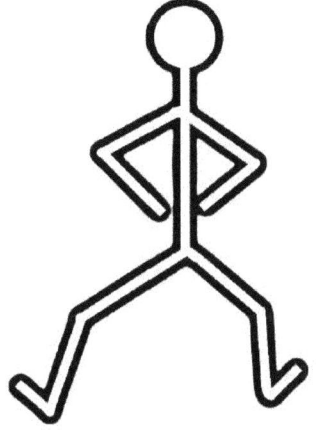

SHAME/GUILT VULNERABILITY

LOVE AND LIGHT ENERGIES

"We are love and light.
There is no beginning and no end.
It comes in its entirety.

Love and light are
freely given and self-perpetuating.

The solid lines of SHAME/GUILT
crack with the intensity of love and light.
The wedge of truth thrusts into the density of falsehoods.

There is no dark side;
it is merely the side that last experienced love and light."[56]

Two groups of individuals exhibit the most SHAME/GUILT vulnerability. The first group includes victims of physical, mental, emotional, or sexual abuse. The second is sensitive individuals. Some persons who occupy both categories are especially susceptible to SHAME/GUILT behavior.

Humanity is an incarnate structure of love and light energies. They are the antitheses of SHAME/GUILT. Love and light energies are the life force of the universe that connects us to everything. They arise from the depth of our souls, and nothing can extinguish them. Love and light, especially self-love, regenerates us.

Love is given freely without cause, and each loving thought we express to ourselves and others counts. We honor ourselves with love when we grace our failures as well as our triumphs. Gratitude helps us find love because it is the window to our soul. It will always return us back to love and light.

Love and light with other positive emotions such as gratitude reinforce our interpersonal bond with steel strength against it. The more love we hold, the stronger our defenses. Our once traumatized persona can reclaim their love and light when they release the SHAME/GUILT. Without its release, we limit ourselves to expand the love we hold. Love and light dissolve the scar of revenge and stops victims from repeating the abuse of the past. We may notice some individuals with severe traumas do not carry revenge or repeat the abuse of the past. We with love and light will triumph over SHAME/ GUILT.

Love is the principle source of wisdom to carry each of us through any night of despair. Love brings forth the heaven frozen in our night. Denial does not exist inside love. Love unites the separated shamed parts of our personality. Love grows in greater quantities. The more we love, the more love we create. When we love we open to ourselves and our soul. Love is the reason for life and the duty of the universe. It is our hope of tomorrow. Love is the expansive quality of the universe. Without it the earth does not spin, and the stars do not dance. Love is our bounty of life.

SENSITIVE PERSONALITIES

Everyone has a lightbody that stores universal love and light energies and the larger the lightbody, the more energies a person can hold. Light is our life force energy or battery. Our light is a continuum of universal light and the many strands of light form our lightbody. The amount of these energies that we maintain is significant in discussing SHAME/ GUILT. Each person has a unique size, and it will either decrease or increase depending on the soul, way of life and the quantity of repressed SHAME/GUILT. Love enlarges the lightbody, and the size of the lightbody regulates the volume of light energy it contains. A sensitive individual has a larger lightbody than a person of a less sensitive nature and can hold more light and love energies. However, the increased amount of love and light energies generates a more reactive nervous system. It makes any sensitive person particularly reactive to oppression and other toxic substances such as chemicals and pharmaceuticals. They may also feel SHAME/GUILT in others, and it pierces the soul with distress. Sensitive individuals feel the untruths hidden in sarcasm and jokes but feels love with an expanded joy that radiates love to others.

Even though sensitivity is a valuable commodity, corporate society frowns upon high levels of emotional sensitivity. The present-day opinion describes a too sensitive person as one who behaves with socially incorrect behavior greater than the average person under similar circumstances. Occasionally, a more sensitive individual may try to negate their sensitive nature with artificial insensitivity. Nonetheless, it is a futile effort. The human structure does not allow the selective denial of feelings without consequence. The soul longs for the nourishment of emotions and senses the abyss of fear without them.

A sensitive child prospers with the guidance of a non-judging, protective parent and frequently fails under a judging, demanding parent. The child's charged nervous system magnifies his emotions and his simple hurts advance into tragedies. A sensitive child feels with depth and reacts with more intensity to emotional pain and oppression than a child of a less sensitive nature. Often society, unaware of this child's needs, erroneously tells parents that their child requires extra discipline to curb his over-reactive nature rather than the guidance of peaceful resolutions.

Sensitive individuals, especially children, show us the value of our feelings. A sensitive child or adult needs to express their spirit because oppression can separate them from their soul, and limit their potential. They may succumb to mediocrity and subsequent unhappiness. If allowed to live the beauty of their spirit or passion, they can capitalize on their enhanced creativity with innovative career choices.

A sensitive person usually seeks emotional healing. They cannot construct an insensitive nature or 'thick skin' and most often internalizes social misunderstandings as their deficiency rather than question others' deceptions. The childlike innocence and lack of SHAME/GUILT understanding often may lead to abusive relationships and the loneliness of self-afflicted unworthiness. A sensitive person is extremely vulnerable to abuse. If they have an excess of SHAME/GUILT, they may quickly tumble into defensive behavior when confronted with the slightest abuse.

A sensitive person has a tougher challenge with SHAME/GUILT, yet has a more resilient defense strategy. Once it is removed love and light energies strengthen the emotional structure. Self-love will maintain a fortress against it. Emotional therapies that include the inner emotional self can help restore the interpersonal bond of self-love.

CHAPTER NINE

SHAME/GUILT MANIFESTATIONS

"**SHAME/GUILT** is powerful because it is
cumulative
adhesive
ubiquitous.
SHAME/GUILT is difficult to define because it is
covert
confusing
distortive
elusive
separative.
SHAME/GUILT is difficult to detect because it is
addictive
habitual
hypnotic
insidious.
SHAME/GUILT is suppressed because it is
irritative
reactive
repulsive."[57]

57   Lois Hollis

ADDICTIVE

Our bodies activate the adrenal glands, which sit atop the kidneys when we experience stress, and we frequently call it fear and excitement. The human body protects itself from these stressors by signaling it to go into a normal fight-or-flight phase. Regardless if the stress is real or imagined; the physiological changes remain the same. Adrenaline and cortisol pour out of the adrenal glands and aid our escape. They contract blood vessels and dilate air passages that increase blood flow to the muscles and oxygen to the lungs. Cortisol supplies the body with adrenaline to raise blood sugar and stimulate fat, protein, and carbohydrate metabolism. They both support the body until it no longer feels threatened. If the stress continues, the overabundance of adrenaline and cortisol imbalances the hormone levels and disease may follow. Especially in the fear state, our bodies generate vast quantities of adrenaline that often leads to a habit or addiction. People exposed to multiple traumas of abuse, internalize this stressor that reinforces their addiction to SHAME/ GUILT behavior and increases their handicap.

In some cultures, addictions to alcohol and euphoric drugs are frequently a defense to intolerable misery, which commonly sources from an abusive past. Not only is SHAME/GUILT at the core of substance addictions, but also it is its equivalent. It distorts the emotional body, and excessive quantities of drugs and alcohol distort the physical body. When a person no longer uses drugs or alcohol but does not heal the emotional body, it will often summon another physical addiction such as sugar.

ADHESIVE

Like a leech, SHAME/GUILT has an adhering quality that increases its size and illusion. Each unresolved offensive incident does not remain isolated within the psyche but rather joins other similar events to construct the SHAME/GUILT repression within our personality.

Some clients reported these feelings that frequently disappeared after they identified and released repressed SHAME/GUILT.

- a gnawing ache in their stomach or heart
- heaviness as if they were carrying a block of cement
- an irritating feeling or slimy sensation
- feeling mummified with layers of blackness
- sensing a black substance, cloud, shadow or circles
- feeling an empty sensation in the abdomen that causes fear

Other clients reported these sensations after releasing SHAME/GUILT.

- a light feeling or a lightening of depression
- more meaningful prayer
- feeling the same peace as felt after hours of meditation
- feeling a larger space within themselves to create their artwork.
- feeling free to do and accomplish anything

One client had written the following poem, "The Black Hole" years before she became aware of SHAME/GUILT.

THE BLACK HOLE

A black hole
in my heart
It is my story.

Fractured pieces
Shattered glass
Hurts that slice with every breath.

It is a part of me.
It is not me.

It seems bigger than me.
It combines with other holes.
It feels larger than the universe.
Through it I feel other holes.
It is an open wound that never seems to heal

It is still a part of me.
It is not me.

I am the love who brings the lessons.
I am the light that makes the hole visible.

I am not the hole.
I am the one who sees the hole.[58]

---

58   Michelle Borderline, letter to author, 21 Jan.2014.

She innocently describes the repressed SHAME/GUILT that created an ethereal hole within her. She feels emptiness, loneliness, and darkness. She honors her emotions and disowns SHAME/GUILT with the words, "It is a part of me but not me." She is correct when she says, "it seems bigger than her." It always gives the illusion of massiveness. She heals herself when she removes it. "I am not the hole. I am the one who sees the hole."

CONFUSION

Confusion is often a sign of SHAME/GUILT behavior that separates us from our healthy awareness and it distorts our logic. We may sense being in a fog, unable to make an informed decision or understand a situation. We often gather more SHAME/GUILT as we blame ourselves for our inability to have clarity. A clandestine organization or individual not willing to publicize their agenda use condescending remarks and other abusive strategies to confuse others. Without identifying SHAME/GUILT as the cause, our temporary confusion may advance into chaos, and we retreat to a victim status. At this time, we can acquiesce to the demands of others.

COVERT

The covert nature of SHAME/GUILT cloaks itself from our awareness in two ways. First, it masks itself, and we live in denial of its existence and second it has the capacity to camouflage itself within our negative states of behavior. Without conscious awareness of its deception, most of us cannot recognize abusive behavior. We, therefore, do not attribute SHAME/GUILT to the cause of emotional disorders or negative emotions. Most of us focus on anxiety, anger, or other negativity instead of it.

CUMULATIVE

"Repressed SHAME/GUILT
gives negative emotions
a sequence of intensity."[59]

SHAME/GUILT has a cumulative property that often incites an unresolved trauma of the past to resurface unexpectedly and turn a simple dispute into a volatile negative reaction. It accumulates within us and supplies the energy force needed to intensify an unexpected negative reaction. The intensity of a negative reaction depends on the quantity of our repression; the greater the amount of repression, the greater the amount of energy available to intensify the negative state. A small quantity of repression will most likely keep us in a low intensity of hurtful feelings whereas a large accumulation can trigger us into an explosive confrontation. The accumulation depends on the type of incident and the sensitivity of the person. We acquire more in a public event than in a private encounter. Continual abuse and the witnessing of a horrific crime can often seed a legacy of SHAME/GUILT, and any sensitive person takes on more regardless of the encounter.

In my experience, I witnessed that a person who has a large quantity of repressed SHAME/GUILT can quickly escalate from hurt into rage and then onto traumatic stress fear, or PTSD. To illustrate how the accumulation intensifies our negativity; I use the emotions of hurt, anxiety, anger, depression, hatred, and fear. The accumulation begins with any abusive incident that causes us to feel hurtful feelings. Without a resolution and with repeated traumas, we will most likely gather more and increase our capacity to experience the state of anxiety. Anxiety is an intense negative emotion that fuels the possibility of future hurts. If the anxiety is unresolved, we will acquire an even greater amount and express anger. Eventually, if our repressed traumas remain without resolution, SHAME/GUILT strengthens into the complex state of depression. The state of depression is a combination of several negative emotions that magnify unworthiness and low self-esteem. Depression may cause a sense of heaviness within the body as we can sometimes sense the weight of negative emotions. Hatred and rage will ultimately manifest as the accumulation increases. If it continues to accumulate, fear will consume us.

SHAME/GUILT STATE OF FEAR

"Fear engulfs me.
The terror of fear is in one piece.

It takes over my breathing making me hollow.
I have nothing to fill me to resist being taken apart.

Dying does not frighten me.
Fear frightens me."[60]

At the onset, fear announces it is a bully. The distortive and cumulative properties of SHAME/GUILT coalesce into the state of fear. Fear distorts our thoughts and emotions into the illusion of traumatic stress fear. Usually, in the fear state we can only think and feel SHAME/GUILT messages of "I have no solution." The fear state encourages more fear, and we are unable to rally any of our positive thoughts for solutions. The intense SHAME/GUILT distortions of negative emotions lock us into catastrophic self-effacing that sustains the debilitating maze of fear delusions. Tragic stories appear in the media demonstrate how additional SHAME/GUILT pushes people past their threshold of resistance and into the abyss of self-annihilation. A sensitive college student, Tyler Clementi, tragically committed suicide after learning that his roommate Ravi Dharun recorded his intimate encounters.[61] Another young man, a high school senior, committed suicide on his prom night after he wrecked his father's Mercedes in an accident. Rather than encounter another abusive incident with his father, he took his life.

Most of us usually try to avoid circumstances that can cause a reenactment of a past trauma. The following story demonstrates how someone, dealing with a manageable amount of SHAME/GUILT fear handles another abusive occurrence.

- Caroline and her only sibling Louise had the task of sorting their father's estate after his untimely death. They decided to share equally. Louise, the younger sister, was unable to

---

60   Lois Hollis journal. 1993.
61   *New York Times*, 16 March, 2012.

travel to her father's hometown, but Caroline was free. Louise compensated Caroline by giving her travel money. Caroline sold the items from their father's house and kept the money without consulting her sister. She told Louise that the items belonged to her because she took the time to travel to their father's home. Louise was furious but unable to confront her older sister. Once again, Caroline conned Louise, and she remains in her childhood paralysis of fear submitting to her sister's desires.

However, if a person endures horrific events such as war and murders they enter the state of traumatic stress fear or PTSD. This state of fear also becomes exaggerated and produces exponential levels of fear that reflexively and continually repeats with a single conscious or unconscious trigger.

PTSD, post-traumatic stress disorder demonstrates the state of fear, and we are grateful to veterans awakening the public to this disorder. When soldiers return home from battle, they reexperience their traumas. They feel as if they are walking through a minefield of trauma triggers. They continue their hypervigilance in their daily activities until they release the SHAME/ GUILT from their inner emotional self. Not wanting to activate their hypervigilant nature they limit social interactions to the point of living in isolation. They consciously and unconsciously avoid trauma triggers that increase the expansive nature of SHAME/GUILT. Often they choose inappropriate behaviors that further increase asocial behavior. Therapies that address the inner emotional self together with knowledge of SHAME/GUILT'S exaggeration, accumulation, and illusion can assist them in recovery.[62]

"Following a trauma that shocks the nervous system beyond its ability to adapt, a person will create a reflex pattern of over-excited behavior. This reflex pattern is a trigger that will fire an abnormal response to a situation, and it automatically continues. To counter the inappropriate behavior, one creates a defense mechanism to avoid certain stimuli or triggers. If a defense is not possible, then one can

---

[62]   Joseph J. Lipari. Underwater Demolition Team 11/Navy Seal. Conversation with
         author.12 Oct. 2015.

exhibit violent behavior. The violent behavior often leads to isolation that society calls antisocial behavior. Many social relationships that include marriage, friendships, and family breakdown and cause depression, exaggerated emotions, night sweats, and the intolerance of self and others. One feels like no one can understand and interpret their distorted inappropriate behaviors. Who could understand their bizarre behavior and who would want to be with them? One feels shamed. They cannot understand or control their feelings and behaviors. Many become homeless or if in a home a recluse. If forced to be social one can exhibit acts of violence to self and others. Traumatic events will build one upon another until life becomes unbearable. I discovered that medications were a temporary fix and had many side effects. Doing shame/ guilt work is the long term solution."[63]

DEFECTIVE

"SHAME/GUILT accumulates in deception
but
it dissolves in detection."[64]

SHAME/GUILT has a cure; it dissolves in detection. It begins to lose its effectiveness as soon as we uncover it. Consider one of the last scenes in the "Wizard of Oz." Dorothy finally reaches the mighty Oz. Terrified with the sounds of the wizard's commanding voice; she stands immovable in front of the wizard's curtain. Her dog, Toto, saves the day when he pulls back the curtain and exposes the wizard. Surprise! The wizard is a short, stout, seemingly unimportant man who broadcasts fear through his megaphone. Dorothy sees the truth. Her fear dissolves and so does the wizard's powers.

---

63   Ibid
64   Ibid

DISTORTIVE

"SHAME/GUILT distorts anything it contacts."[65]

SHAME/GUILT distorts whatever it contacts, and, therefore it will alter that particular object similar to the way a virus corrupts a computer. The devastation that it can create depends on the importance of the object it influences.

Awareness of the following two conditions can help us realize the enormous distortion and eventual destruction that it exerts upon our lives. The first condition is the awareness of the interconnectedness of our physical, mental, emotional, and spiritual fields that also connect with our environment and the universe. The second is the significance of our nervous system that includes the brain to direct our life force energy throughout the interconnectedness of our energy fields.

PERSONAL INTERCONNECTEDNESS

"A human being is a part of a whole, called by us universe, a part limited in time and space. He experiences himself, his thoughts and feelings as something separated from the rest... a kind of optical delusion of his consciousness. This delusion is a kind of prison for us, restricting us to our personal desires and affection for a few persons nearest to us. Our task must be to free ourselves from this prison by widening our circle of compassion to embrace all living creatures and the whole of nature in its beauty."[66]

We have physical, mental, emotional, and spiritual energy fields or parts that make up our human physicality that gives us the ability to enjoy our presence within the world and evolve. Without each system or body, we remain dormant. Our physical body houses organs and their systems. Our mental body creates and processes thought while maintaining our belief

---

65   Lois Hollis
66   Albert Einstein Quote

structure. Our emotional body communicates our feelings and connects us to our soul. The many spiritual parts connect us with the realm of soul and the universe.

Each one of our bodies is interrelated and interdependent. Their interconnectedness creates our unique invisible field or aura that influences our behavior. We often study a particular part for its properties, but a myopic view may overshadow our interconnectedness. We are the sum of our various parts or energy fields. No part is superior to the other, and any experience either positive or negative in one part will impact the other.

NERVOUS SYSTEM

Our nervous system is our transport system. It directs life force energy from our spiritual intelligence throughout our interconnectedness to supply functional information, thought, and emotion. The nervous system transports and transmits anatomical and physiological instructions to and from each organ, thought, and emotion. Subsequently our heart beats, lungs breathe; emotions feel, mind thinks, and our soul connects with God or spirit. We automatically complete a sophisticated system of giving and receiving. Our seemingly invisible aura is the continuous flow of our interconnected energy. It ascends the energy pathway within our physical, emotional, mental, and spiritual fields advancing to universal consciousness. It then descends from universal or cosmic consciousness to our individual energy fields.[67]

Our nervous system contains trillions of nerve cells. Each nerve cell individually vibrates with our life force energy. The nervous system is alive and its rhythmic language of nerve cell vibration maintains our life force. Sometimes we can sense our life force as chills throughout our body. "Nerve vibration creates consciousness and makes possible life itself."[68] The nervous system regulates the vibrations of our nerves, in a similar manner that the strings of a violin transmit the tone of music. If the nerves or violin strings are too tight or loose, they will not be in balance and convey the incorrect tone of music. "When our nerves alter their tension they vibrate

---

67   Daniel David Palmer, *The Chiropractor 1914*, (Los Angeles: Beacon Light Printing, 1914,17-21.
68   Ibid,18.

out of their tone. Pain is the result of nerves out of tone because they are too tight, and nerves that are too lax lose their sensation."[69]

The skeletal structure provides the doctor of chiropractic the means to adjust bones and return the nervous system to its normal tone of health. Now, I understand how I was able to visualize my repressed childhood memory after a chiropractic adjustment. In a sense, the adjustment balanced my nervous system or took it out of distortion. Then, my innate intelligence could release the repressed childhood image.

Nerve vibration and our interconnectedness help us understand how the energy of SHAME/GUILT can distort our nervous system and cause physical, mental, and emotional disorders. When our nervous system vibrates with its correct tone or rhythm; it sends healthy impulses to our physical, mental, emotional and spiritual bodies. We live in the flow of life. When our nervous system sends distortive or faulty signals throughout our interconnectedness, we can develop disease. Similarly, when a virus sends out corrupted signals throughout a computer, it malfunctions.

Society and the medical profession unknowingly but correctly labels the lack of healthy tone within the nervous system as stress. Stress is the abnormal nerve vibrational pattern within the nervous system that precipitates the physical, mental, emotional, or spiritual distortions of disease. Any stressor, trauma, toxin or autosuggestion takes our body out of its normal tone of nerve vibration, and we can develop the emotional or physical pain of stress leading to disease.[70] Autosuggestions distort our nervous system. Autosuggestion is what we do, say, and think to ourselves and others that will send either unhealthy or healthy messages within us.

> **Repeated SHAME/GUILT statements of "I am guilty, or I am worthless" distort or alter our vibrational nerve tone and send unhealthy messages that can contribute to disease. Healthy suggestions of "I am doing a great job, or I am a good person" vibrate balanced tones that keep us in health.**

---

69   Joseph J. Lipari, DC., conversation with author, 22 Oct. 2011.
70   Daniel David Palmer, The Chiropractor 1914, (Los Angeles: Beacon Light Printing, 1914),25.

Trauma and toxic substances, such as the ingestion of putrefied food, toxic chemicals, and some pharmaceuticals can also unbalance our nervous system and transmit unhealthy distortions otherwise known as side effects.

Behavior is not a series of random events. "The real and direct cause of disease is more or less nerve tension than normal."[71] **SHAME/GUILT distorts the nervous system and alters its tone.** It expertly takes advantage of the synergistic nature of our nervous system and dedicated lines of communication throughout our interconnectedness. It embeds within the nervous system and sickens our body and crushes our spirit.

SHAME/GUILT is a foreign substance that produces stress similar to any other toxic material. Our human physiology has no familiarity with it and, as a result, has no ability to assimilate it. Out of options, we store it similar to any other toxin, and it accumulates into our repression. Typically the nervous system adapts to unhealthy substances that cause stress, but the scar of traumas continues to broadcast its distortive signal. Prolonged distortive influences lead us out of our balance of health and into emotional and physical disorders. The nervous system will transmit the distorted signals until we release it; likewise a computer infected with a virus will send corrupted data until we remove the virus.

THINKING VERSUS FEELING EMOTIONS

**"Thoughts and feelings coexist
as if they were inside each other.
Together they create a line of consciousness."[72]**

SHAME/GUILT distorts our emotions and blocks us from feeling which gives us the tendency to think rather than feel. Considering that healing comes through the emotions, thinking our emotions will delay our recovery. "Although ours is generally considered a rational brain," Kenneth Wesson says, "it is an emotional brain, where feelings receive first priority."[73]

71   Ibid, 23.
72   Lois Hollis
73   Dr. Kenneth Wesson, "Brain Sight:: Can touch allow us to see better than sight?" *Brain*

SHAME AND GUILT ARE NEVER HEALTHY

Healthy shame and healthy guilt are oxymorons. SHAME/GUILT distorts our mental abilities, and we cleverly rationalize them as healthy. Some people proclaim that shame and guilt are necessary to keep us responsible for our actions, preserve morality, and decrease lawlessness. To the contrary, they intensify violence, disempowerment, stress, and hate. They keep us stuck in our dysfunctional personality which reduces our ability to succeed, evolve, and love. They can also predispose our bodies to physical disease by stressing the immune system and causing inflammation.[74]

JUST BE POSITIVE

> "More than we know or choose to admit,
> our past unresolved SHAME/GUILT experiences
> shape our present behavior."[75]

The ability to maintain a positive approach has helped many overcome a harmful situation, but SHAME/GUILT can also distort the expression "Just Be Positive." Positive exaggerated thinking is the mask of denial that creates imbalances within us. It can deplete our life force energy as we continue to use our positive messages to battle our abusive messages. We may deny our unresolved emotional issues, but denial cannot stop the emotional pain. Nor does it allow us to recognize our fullest potential. SHAME/GUILT often holds our greatest gifts captive even though we surround ourselves with positive thoughts.

World Magazine, March 1, 2012.

74   Sally S.Dickerson MA, Margaret E. Kemeny, PHD, Najb Aziz, MD, Kevin H. Kim, PHD, and John L. Fahey, MD. "Immunological Effects of Induced Shame and Guilt." *Psychosomatic Medicine* 66:124–131 (2004).

75   Lois Hollis

ELUSIVE

The academia of psychology's plethora of disorders keeps us circling around SHAME/GUILT but never arriving at it. It is elusive, subtle, mysterious, seemingly invisible, and difficult to define. Some sources classify shame into classifications such as; present, past, individual, societal, group, public, genuine, false, secret, and toxic. Others describe good shame and bad shame as well as good guilt and bad guilt. Lynne Namka, Ed.D. writes, "loss of function shame rage, guilt piling up shame rage."[76] These subgroups identify abusive behavior but not its location. If we add its location, we can more easily unmask it. We can reclassify it with the emotion that it attaches onto such as the SHAME/GUILT of anger, the SHAME/GUILT of anxiety, and so on. This reclassification will increase our chances of detecting it and our ability to release it.

HABITUAL - HYPNOTIC

"Guilt repeats the voice of shame that echoes our unworthiness."[77]

SHAME/GUILT HYPNOSIS

Shame uses our unconscious voice and guilt uses our conscious awareness. Either way the critical voice of unworthiness continues day and night that activates a trance-like state of hypnosis. The trance state of hypnosis is a powerful state of consciousness. It makes our minds susceptible to commands. The critical thoughts from our SHAME/GUILT inner critic's voice easily embed within us. Even though we consciously try to deflect them, they still enter our mind. Anyone or culture with coercive agendas such as gangs, cults, and organized crime broadcast abusive statements to exploit the trance state of hypnosis.

---

76 Lynne Namka, Ed.D.,http://www.angeriesout.com (accessed 02 Oct.2013).
77 Lois Hollis

- Let us compare SHAME/GUILT to the tale of Sleeping Beauty. Instead of pricking our finger on a spinning wheel, we pierce it on an abusive incident. The SHAME/GUILT poison enters our nervous system and proliferates into the layers of our interconnectedness. It blackens our healthy emotions and thoughts to create the hypnotic trance of unworthiness and fear. Sleeping Beauty, our logical mind goes to sleep, and SHAME/GUILT controls us with its hypnotic trance. We awaken to our worthiness when we discover our inner self. We, the conscious healthy self who is the Prince Charming of this tale accept our inner self of troubled emotions with a kiss of love. Our emotions awaken to their love and beauty and remove the SHAME/GUILT they carry. We with our kingdom of self live happily ever after. It is highly unlikely that a single abusive event would place anyone into a hypnotic trance. Nevertheless, this tale can help us comprehend the dangers of the hypnotic power of SHAME/GUILT.

THE SHAME/GUILT QUOTA
RECURRING SHAME/GUILT

**"The amount of SHAME/GUILT we experience
equals
the amount we repressed."[78]**

The SHAME/GUILT quota is the primary reason we are unable to detach from guilt and shame or liberate ourselves from addictions mainly drugs and alcohol. In my experience, I witnessed that the amount of abuse we encounter equals the amount we repressed. Our inner critic, the **SHAME/ GUILT producer**, has the responsibility to maintain this balance. With infinite diligence, he will use any negativity to broadcast defeat to correct an imbalance. He will cause excessive guilt, failure, resentment, protracted grief, and self-judgments that he learned from the culture, parents, and other authorities. Procrastination is the most subtle that can lead to self-sabotage. Our inner critic, the master of SHAME/ GUILT, perfectly duplicates our childhood and adolescent abuse that can develop into our adult behavior.

We threaten our inner critic when we desire personal or career advancements and our critic will retaliate with self-sabotaging behavior to maintain its balance. He will block our efforts because his purpose is to protect us from emotional hurts. However, keeping us emotionally safe does not allow us the expansion to evolve and reach our goals. Resolution happens when we decrease the amount of SHAME/GUILT we had repressed which will reduce the amount our inner critic must produce. Simultaneously we must learn to reject any new abuse, especially judgmental self-abuse. In the end, the critic creates less negativity. With a harmonious relationship, we and our inner critic or SHAME/GUILT producer will realize that the resolution of our emotional dilemmas comes from not giving or accepting abuse.

---

78   Lois Hollis

IRRITATIVE

**"SHAME/GUILT is an irritant and toxin
that deposits within us
to produce stress
leading to inflammation and
ultimately to disorders."[79]**

There is a growing body of scientific evidence that is now linking stress to chronic inflammation. Stress keeps our immune system on high alert. Sheldon Cohen states "research shows for the first time that the effects of psychological stress on the body's ability to regulate inflammation can promote the development and progression of disease. When under stress cells of the immune system are unable to respond to hormonal control, and consequently, produce levels of inflammation that promotes disease. Because inflammation plays a role in many diseases such as cardiovascular, asthma and autoimmune disorders, this model suggests why stress impacts them as well."[80]

SHAME/GUILT is not only a stressor, but it is also an irritant. Any abusive event that we encounter produces an irritant that scars our inner emotional self. Unless we resolve the abusive incident, the scar remains and continues to produce stress. It will also generate additional SHAME/GUILT when we re-experience another abusive incident or self-imposed defaming thoughts.

The judicial system of earlier years and in some cultures today requires people who broke the law to wear a badge of shame and parade in a public place. This behavior produces large quantities of SHAME/GUILT and escalates hatred and anger. How interesting that the mark or shame badge mirrors the scar within our inner emotional self.

---

79   Lois Hollis

80   Sheldon Cohen Carnegie Mellon University. "How stress influences disease: Study reveals inflammation as the culprit." *ScienceDaily*. www.sciencedaily.com/releases/2012/04/120402162546. htm (accessed May 5, 2015).

REACTIVE

SHAME/GUILT REFLEX RESPONSE

Emotions are also considered reflexes and they function with SHAME/GUILT within our involuntary unconscious nervous system to produce distorted behaviors.[81]

An emotional or physical reflex response is either healthy or unhealthy. Our behavior is healthy when we take our hand off a hot stove and unhealthy when we have a temper tantrum for missing our favorite movie. Without a resolution, SHAME/GUILT disrupts or distorts normal nerve tone vibrations and constructs an unhealthy reflex response circuit. The unhealthy loop of behavior begins with a traumatic episode of abuse. It produces specific physical and emotional behaviors that replay with predictability whenever a person re-experiences a similar trauma.

For instance; Sally quickly gets frustrated when she cannot solve a technical problem with her computer. Her frustration immediately turns to unworthiness and then to tears. Each new unresolved attack increases the SHAME/ GUILT energy that intensifies subsequent reactions. Over time, it is possible for us to experience an overdramatic reaction to a minor abusive incident.

SHAME/GUILT TRIGGER

A SHAME/GUILT reflex response is an involuntary pattern of behavior in response to a trigger. A trigger is a precise word or behavior that activates a physical and emotional reflex response. Everyone has distinct triggers because of our unique experiences. They activate our most vulnerable trait or the emotion that retains the largest quantity of repressed SHAME/GUILT. Some may say it is our Achilles' heel. Each distortion represents a category of unresolved issues such as; work performance, parenting, writing, cooking, money, body image, in addition to any negative emotion. Unresolved issues remain dormant within our repressed distortions and await a trigger to unleash their fury. If we have anger tendencies, the SHAME/GUILT of

---

81   Dr. Joseph Lipari, DC, conversation with author, 18 Feb.2013.

our anger will ignite, and we will sense a rage gushing through our body. If we have a tendency to despondency, our trigger could activate depression. The following story describes a typical reflex response.

- Steven participates in a friendly game of tennis doubles at his company's picnic. During the match, his partner accidentally bumps into him as he runs for the ball. After a few humorous spins, Steven loses his balance and flips onto the ground with the audience's laughter. He immediately stands and brushes the dirt off his white tennis shorts, but he does not share the humor. Head down in a profuse sweat of embarrassment, he exits the tennis court even though he has no physical injuries. Steven's minor fall activates his old hurtful trauma of being unable to speak up in his defense. In grade school, Steven was unable to confront the class bullies when they knocked him off his bike in front of other classmates. Without comment, Steven immediately returned to his bike and peddled home with the echoes of sneering laughter. He never fought back or reported the attacks to his teachers or parents. With each new attack, Steven added more SHAME/GUILT, which further reduced his already low self-esteem. His silent rage commands him now to walk away from another suggestion of humiliation.

The following account demonstrates how a new abusive incident brought a person into confusion because of a large amount of repression.

- Driving through an intersection, Gary heard someone hit the rear of his car. Stunned, he stopped to meet the driver of the other car. Russell, a tall, obese man, screams "You hit my car" as he approaches Gary while talking to the police on his cell phone. Gary instinctively apologized, but Russell continued to talk on his cell phone. At that time, Gary could not remember the sound of the cars colliding and apologized once again for the accident. When the police arrived on the scene, Russell cornered the officer and pointed to a small scrape on the side of his truck and old damage on the front of Gary's car. The police supervised their exchange of insurance information and then ticketed Gary. Russell and the police left the scene.

Confused, Gary sat quietly in his car unable to find a resolution; he called his friend and explained the accident. His friend said, "A good defense is a good offense." Gary now considered the possibility that Russell caused the accident but blamed him. Gary closed his eyes and tried once again to remember the details. This time, he remembered hearing Russell's car hit the back of his car! Gary realized that he could not remember the original bang on the back of his car when Russell shouted at him and blamed him for the accident.

SHAME/GUILT can produce forgetfulness, confusion, and even shortterm amnesia. Our minds in the interest of self-preservation help us forget past traumas. Gary was unable to recall the details of the accident because Russell triggered his repressed abusive childhood. Often Gary's parents wrongfully punished him for the destructive pranks of his older sister. They usually took her side, and he was unable to defend himself. Gary now could connect the SHAME/GUILT from Russell's wrongful blaming to the abuse from his parents. Gary released the SHAME/GUILT from his parents, sister, and Russell. He also made the decision not to accept the responsibility or blame for others' misfortunes.

Luckily, most people tiptoe in and out of traumatic events, and their reflex responses last only a few minutes and without disorientation. Nevertheless, an emotionally compromised individual struggling with considerable SHAME/GUILT may lack the innate resources to cope successfully and require professional guidance.

REPULSIVE

Not easily discussed, understood or felt, SHAME/GUILT preserves its secrecy with the help of the oblivion of our handicap and society's conditioning. It truly is the thief in the night who robs us of self-esteem. Its power comes from our unwillingness to acknowledge it. As most of us know, it makes us feel disgusting, sad, angry, depressed, and many other negative states. Why would we want to have those feelings? In fact, we want to deny our association with it. Sad to say, we live in shame's shadow. Any SHAME/ GUILT culture humiliates us if we use the word shame and this will intensify our personal disgust. We repress our feelings and do not want to expose our secret traumas and unworthiness. Our handicap accommodates our false protection with a sudden burst of repulsion that instantly renounces the word shame or any experience that elicits it. Some individuals take great measures to avoid it and may exhibit self-destructive behaviors such as eating disorders, addictions, self-injury, and even suicide attempts. Some organizations use the repulsive nature of SHAME/GUILT onto their workforce as a negative incentive to increase productivity. Competition is a healthy incentive, but it takes on an unhealthy tone of bullying when a company interjects it. Employees' achievements frequently and publically posted within the company, academic grades displayed on school bulletin boards, and public shaming will only produce short term results since they activate more SHAME/GUILT for everyone not only the victims.

SEPARATIVE

> "We sit beside ourselves
> separated from our hearts and minds
> until we sit within ourselves."[82]

SHAME/GUILT by its presence separates or dissociates us from our logical healthy emotions and thoughts. Unknowingly, we behave and think with the distorted part of our personality. At this time, we relive the emotional isolation of our traumas with our distorted emotions and thoughts. SHAME/GUILT separates:

- each abusive event from the other.
- the connectedness of our energy fields and lessens our life force.
- our healthy self and gives us the illusion of abandonment.
- the bond between self, others, parents, and their children.

---

82   Lois Hollis

- people with racial prejudice.
- us from our needs. We may feel too unworthy to nourish ourselves and instead support others. Alternatively, we may feel superior to our fellow man and refuse to offer support.

Some meditative practices that disown or escape uncomfortable negative feelings have the tendency to increase SHAME/GUILT, and therefore, deepen the separation or dissociation within the personality. Conversely, a meditative practice that honors both positive and negative emotions may help decrease the separations.

UBIQUITOUS

Behavior, right or wrong, follows everyone in the evolutionary matrix. SHAME/GUILT is ubiquitous, ever-present everywhere because it permeates the ethers[83] and diffuses into the collective unconscious.[84] If we search deep enough within our inner emotional self, we will discover how it orchestrates life.

"The light of knowledge and love are ubiquitous.

Truth illuminates secrecy and
pierces the SHAME/GUILT of servitude, and
many awaken to the damages of abusive behavior.

Evolutionary love and light energies
continuously guide us on our journey
away from SHAME/GUILT and
towards our innate moral sense."[85]

---

83 Ethers are the elastic substance or medium filling all spaces, by which molecular vibrations of light, gravity, mental telepathy and other natural phenomena can travel and penetrate all substances. Daniel David Palmer, The Chiropractor 1914, (Los Angeles: Beacon Light Printing,1914),20.
84 Jungianpsychology. inborn unconscious psychic material common to humankind, accumulated by the experience of all preceding generations. http://www.thefreedictionary.com/collective+unconscious.
85 Lois Hollis

PART THREE

SHAME /GUILT RECOVERY

CHAPTER TEN

CLIMBING OUT OF SHAME / GUILT

> "Wisdom is the giver of truth
> blossomed by love and
> brought forth by desire."[86]

TWELVE SHAME/GUILT ALERTS™

I have listed twelve alerts to help you keep a mindfulness of SHAME/GUILT so that you can break through its hypnosis and discover your treasure of creativity, self-love, and innate genius to live with individuality, vulnerability, and compassion. The key to immunity is the knowledge of its trickery, an interpersonal bond with your inner emotional self as well as others, and a continual decrease in SHAME/GUILT repression or handicap.

ALERT #1

**We can benefit from the
appropriate use of
the words shame and guilt.**

The repetitive and incorrect usage of the words shame and guilt can keep you stuck in its trap. Words influence your behavior and the more you use them, the greater their impact. If you continue to communicate with shame and guilt inappropriately, you train your mind and, therefore, yourself to accept abuse. It is more accurate and beneficial to speak words that accurately express your feelings or situations rather than connecting yourself to SHAME/GUILT. The word shame is often used to imply sadness for a crime against innocent victims. It implies that perpetrators should feel shame and suffer for their wrongdoings. The statement, "It is a shame that the robbers killed the innocent children" or "It is such a shame that you lost the game" can more accurately represent your feelings if you change the wording. Instead of using the expression it is a shame, to express sadness or want retribution, you can say; it is appalling, disgraceful, disastrous, unfortunate, or so sad. The phrase, to my sorrow or I am heartbroken over the tragedy can also be effective. Guilt-free desserts are a popular food category, but it subliminally deepens the connection to food and guilt. Often your subconscious mind interprets the guilt-free as guilt. Perhaps you can replace guilt-free with the words healthy, nutritious, wholesome, or any other to express health, not guilt. In contrast, it is necessary to use the words shame and guilt in healing and personal growth. The avoidance of recognizing abusive behavior and releasing it, again keeps us in its trap. Once you identify it by its correct name and call it out of hiding, SHAME/GUILT begins to lose its power.

ALERT #2

SHAME/GUILT sabotages emotional healing.

SHAME/GUILT intimidates you. When you begin to feel your emotions, you most likely will feel the influence of SHAME/GUILT not your emotions. Perhaps your first encounter with it was in childhood and at that time it frightened you. Now as an adult you relive those fearful events through your child memories, not as a knowledgeable adult. Today, your adult self can help your child self of the past to release the SHAME/GUILT that he or she still carries.

ALERT #3

Personal growth and healing are life-long endeavors.

**The hypnosis of SHAME/GUILT
lulls your mind into a false sense of health.**

SHAME/GUILT mindfulness must be ongoing. Repressed SHAME/GUILT arises in layers, and you uncover it like a mummy, one layer at a time. The smallest release of it can shift you into unexpected joy, and you may feel that additional emotional introspection seems unnecessary. However, a SHAME/GUILT culture can successfully delude anyone from their initial triumphs of healed traumas and use your complacency to reinforce its control. Your initial shifts of joy are merely a glimpse of what you can ultimately achieve. Practice will help you identify and release SHAME/GUILT quickly with ease.

ALERT #4

**Knowledge—Training—Practice--Healing
are the keys
that will help you repel the tricky behavior of SHAME/GUILT.**

Knowledge alone will not give you the competitive edge over SHAME/GUILT. The practice of emotional protection statements and a mindfulness of its manifestations will give you the ability to quickly site an abusive situation and proceed with a neutral reply. However, healing your emotions and releasing the SHAME/GUILT within your inner self will bring the most effective and lasting means to win over abuse.

ALERT #5

SHAME/GUILT Diary

**GIVE NO SHAME/GUILT
ACCEPT NO SHAME/GUILT**

SHAME/GUILT probably slithers by most of us discounted and ignored. In fact, it is so tricky that it can take up to several years to realize that you experienced an encounter. A personal log that details how you identified and released the SHAME/GUILT from any new or old trauma can accelerate your recovery and resilience. Include the following in your diary:

- Date your SHAME/GUILT experiences.
- What words or situation triggered the experience?
- How did you initially respond?
- Is there a more appropriate way to respond?
- Give yourself inner hugs often. Thanking yourself brings gratitude.

ALERT #6

**The retracing response is healing,
not regressing back into dysfunction.**

Retracing is a natural response that occurs with holistic healing and is often considered a healing crisis. In your emotional healing, you will unavoidably but quickly re-visit or retrace the abusive situation that caused the SHAME/GUILT. You must find the SHAME/GUILT to release it. At this time, you can let it go. For example; driving by car to a specific location you notice landmarks. You will re-experience the same landmarks on your return but in the reverse order.

ALERT #7

Avoid the thinking trap.

**The hypnosis of SHAME/GUILT teaches you to
think rather than feel your emotions.**

SHAME/GUILT conditions you to think and analyze your feelings with an observational attitude. The mind does not like surprises, and quite often shows you what you want to know, rather than your truth. Emotional health happens through your emotions, but SHAME/GUILT takes you away from feeling. It uses denial to lock you into the thinking trap. Without a resolution, the cycle of thinking perpetuates itself, and SHAME/GUILT accumulates while increasing your inability to feel.

ALERT #8

SHAME/GUILT awareness
quickens recovery and healing.

The health care industry may consider addressing SHAME/GUILT in their therapies as a way to quicken the recovery of their clients. Hospice and similar end-of-life programs may especially reference it to assist others to leave the physical existence in their most enlightened state.

ALERT #9

SHAME/GUILT is not yours to own.

Refrain from owning shame or guilt. SHAME/GUILT is not yours to own, and you can release it. Hidden SHAME/GUILT is easy to release but tricky to locate. Occasionally you can spontaneously release some in the retelling of traumatic events, but the release is usually incomplete with the possibility of transferring it to another person. The statement "I release all SHAME/GUILT" is also ineffective. It releases when you have a clear awareness of it. Sometimes it is best to ask permission from your inner self to remove it because a part of you may still need its protection of secrecy.

- Acknowledge and identify SHAME/GUILT.
- Close your eyes and feel or see the SHAME/GUILT covering you or within your inner self.
- Separate from it.
- You can use the force of your energy to remove it from your inner vision and return it to your abuser or the universe to dissolve.

ALERT #10

The balance and strength of your combined physical, mental, emotional, and spiritual bodies will bring you into sustained health.

SHAME/GUILT distorts all aspects of our interconnectedness. Since each part has the same importance, they need individual recovery. We can heal our physical bodies with the proper nutritional balance of vital mineral, vitamins, protein, fats, carbohydrates, in addition to a release of toxins. We can love our inner self into healing with the release of repressed SHAME/ GUILT that it holds. Our inner self can dissolve past beliefs that limit potential and establish beliefs that empower. Nature and the aliveness of life can nourish our souls.

ALERT #11

**Use the innate wisdom of your soul as a motivator
not
the consequences of SHAME/GUILT.**

SHAME/GUILT will have less control over your life the more you can make decisions from your innate wisdom. You can use your innate sense to guide your behavior, not the consequences of SHAME/GUILT. "I feel guilty if I do not help" can evolve into "I feel to help because it is the right thing for me to do." SHAME/GUILT lessens when you naturally live your destined soul work for the betterment of humanity.

ALERT #12

**Build a support system.
Find a SHAME/GUILT Buddy.
Create a SHAME/GUILT Healing Group.**

At this time, SHAME/GUILT can easily and quickly deceive you. Even though you are knowledgeable, you will most likely need the support of another to identify the subtleties of it. A support group and a buddy familiar with this knowledge can assist you in identifying abusive behavior. Your support system can also create a safety net that will provide protection from emotional isolation, help restore your interpersonal bond, and share innovative ways of non-abusive communication. As with any group, each participant must have confidentiality and no judgment.

**Without SHAME/GUILT leaching,
the universe expands
with our personal expansion
and
every particle of life evolves.**

**I believe humanity will evolve from SHAME/GUILT repression
into a collective compassion that
will
spiral into the universe
and
bring heaven to earth.**

FURTHER WORKS

Thank you for joining me on this SHAME/GUILT adventure. We have reached the end of these pages, but we have not reached the end of the journey. Re-reading this book and having it in sight as a source will help maintain the mindfulness necessary to free yourself from the shackles of SHAME/GUILT.

Please feel free to contact me at soulspeaks@hotmail.com.

I welcome with appreciation your feedback or questions as you practice this new knowledge to identify and release SHAME/GUILT from your lives. Meet me online. My website will keep you informed of books, videos, workshops, in addition to my newsletter and blog for new information. I will also share techniques to resolve abusive experiences and how to create a SHAME/GUILT support group and buddy system.

www.loishollis.com
www.soulspeaks.net

Experience my other products that can guide you to self-love and awaken the divinity of soul to heal and expand your creativity.

"Out of Discord Into Harmony" DVD takes place in the unconscious mind to illustrate how the SHAME/GUILT of negative emotions hides your power and passion.

"Soul Mirror Cards" are abridged poetic verses of universal consciousness that bring you intuitive insights.

"The Universe Speaks" book, written in the language of the soul helps awaken you to your purpose and nourish your soul.

DVD Series with Workbook designed to help you identify and release SHAME/GUILT.

www.ingramcontent.com/pod-product-compliance
Lightning Source LLC
Chambersburg PA
CBHW051214120626
46547CB00013B/1351